Brilliant Activities for

Reading Comprehension, Year 6

Engaging Stories and Activities to Develop Comprehension Skills

Charlotte Makhlouf

Brilliant
PUBLICATIONS

Brilliant Publications Limited publishes many other practical resource books for primary school teachers, a few of which are listed below. You will find more details on our website: www.brilliantpublications.co.uk.

Brilliant Activities for Reading Comprehension Series

Year 1 978-1-78317-070-8
Year 2 978-1-78317-071-5
Year 3 978-1-78317-072-2
Year 4 978-1-78317-073-9
Year 5 978-1-78317-074-6

Brilliant Activities for Creative Writing Series

Year 1 978-0-85747-463-6
Year 2 978-0-85747-464-3
Year 3 978-0-85747-465-0
Year 4 978-0-85747-466-7
Year 5 978-0-85747-467-4
Year 6 978-0-85747-468-1

Boost Creative Writing Series

Years 1–2 978-1-78317-058-6
Years 3–4 978-1-78317-059-3
Years 5–6 978-1-78317-060-9

Published by Brilliant Publications Limited
Unit 10
Sparrow Hall Farm
Edlesborough
Dunstable
Bedfordshire
LU6 2ES, UK

Tel: 01525 222292

E-mail: info@brilliantpublications.co.uk

Website: www.brilliantpublications.co.uk

The name Brilliant Publications and the logo are registered trademarks.

Written by Charlotte Makhlouf

Illustrated by Calvin Innes, Pat Murray and Frank Endersby

Cover illustration by Frank Endersby

Front cover designed by Brilliant Publications Limited

© Text: Charlotte Makhlouf 2012, revised and updated 2014

© Design: Brilliant Publications Limited 2012, revised and updated 2014

ISBN: 978-1-78317-075-3

e-book ISBN: 978-1-78317-082-1

This second edition was first printed and published in the UK in 2014

The right of Charlotte Makhlouf to be identified as the author of this work has been asserted by herself in accordance with the Copyright, Designs and Patents Act 1988.

Contents

Introduction

The importance of reading for meaning should never be underestimated. Whilst many young children might be able to decode quite complex texts, it is vital that they understand what they read. More importantly, it is fundamental that they enjoy what they are reading.

Over my 15 years of experience, I have used a number of comprehension books as part of my English teaching. Very few of them have engaged the children who are being asked to read and understand them. I decided that if we are asking children to read, understand and answer questions from a passage, that passage should at least engage their attention, and indeed their teacher's attention as well.

The passages in the **Brilliant Activities for Reading Comprehension Series** are designed to give children valuable reading practice through varied, enjoyable texts. The passages begin in the **Year 1** book with simple picture comprehension. They gradually increase in difficulty as you progress through the book, and through the series, encouraging pupils to use a range of decoding strategies and to develop their ability to read for meaning. The passages are entirely fictional and it is hoped that both pupils and teachers will find them humorous.

Teachers should read the texts with the children and discuss them thoroughly before allowing them to proceed to the activities. If you are using the e-book version, you can display the pages on the interactive white board.

In the **Year 6** book there are first a series of Questions that require factual recall. Encourage children to respond in full sentences. The Word work sections will help to develop and stretch their vocabulary. The Extension work sections require more open-ended answers enabling the pupils to provide a more personal response. Children should write the answers in their workbooks or on separate sheets of paper. Answers are provided on pages 122–141. On pages 8–19 there are some suggestions for ways in which the passages can be linked to writing, speaking and other literacy activities, as well as to other areas of the curriculum. These activities are ideal for children who finish their work early.

The **Brilliant Activities for Reading Comprehension Series** provides the teacher with a basis for ensuring progression. The activities give pupils:

◆ the ability to select or retrieve information in order to answer the questions successfully using a full sentence

◆ the opportunity to deduce, infer or interpret information, events or ideas from the texts

◆ the opportunity to identify and comment on the structure and organisation of the text and comment on the writer's use of language at word and sentence level

◆ the chance to comment on cultural, social or historical traditions and the impact the text may have on the reader.

The **Brilliant Activities for Reading Comprehension Series** provides an invaluable resource for assessing pupil progress in reading. The chart on pages 5–7 shows how the activities link to the relevant Programmes of Study in the National Curriculum for England (September 2014).

Links to the National Curriculum

Pupils should be taught to	
maintain positive attitudes to reading and understanding of what they read by:	
continuing to read and discuss an increasingly wide range of fiction, poetry, plays, non-fiction and reference books or textbooks	A wide range of different types of fiction and non-fiction writing are covered in the book. The passages have been written to engage pupils' attention and these help to promote positive attitudes to reading. Have class debates and discussions on books they have read. Discuss major themes arising. Pupils should continue to apply the knowledge and skills they have already learnt to more complex writing. Even though pupils can now read independently, reading aloud to them is still important and should include whole books so that they meet books and authors that they might not choose to read themselves.
reading books that are structured in different ways and reading for a range of purposes	Through reading and analysing the passages in this book, pupils will learn that text is structured in different ways, depending on the purpose of the writing. In addition to using the passages in this book, pupils should be given the opportunity to read a wide variety of books of different types. Continue to explore different texts by reading journals and newspapers and discussing current affairs. Compare and contrast texts.
increasing their familiarity with a wide range of books, including myths, legends and traditional stories, modern fiction, fiction from our literary heritage, and books from other cultures and traditions	Ensure the pupils know the specific criteria which make a story a myth or legend. Look at Old English texts and Shakespeare texts to see/ evaluate how language has changed.
recommending books that they have read to their peers, giving reasons for their choices	Have a book reading group or a public speaking debate on books where they compare/contrast texts and recommend a favourite.
identifying themes and conventions in a wide range of writing	Pupils should be taught to recognise themes in what they read, such as loss or heroism. They should have opportunities to compare characters, consider different accounts of the same event and discuss viewpoints (both of authors and fictional characters), within a text and across more than one text.

identifying themes and conventions in a wide range of writing (cont)	Examples of themes covered in this book include: Autumn (page 32) – thankfulness; Feral Cats (page 41) – loyalty; Snegworthy (page 62) – coping with fear/unknown; The Dark Side (page 83) – homelessness; The Organisation (page 103) – fear; The Viking Raid (page 111) – revenge/ courage. Pupils should continue to learn the conventions of different types of writing, such as the use of the first person in writing diaries and autobiographies. Examples of conventions used in this book include: diary format – Game Ranger Diaries (page 44); play script – The Formula – part 1 (page 90) and part 2 (page 93); letter format – A Sojourn in Bath (page 23); newspaper/magazine articles – Stately Homes (page 47), Shopping Centre Opens (page 80) and Virus on Space Station (page 119).
making comparisons within and across books	Compare and contrast the different passages in this book. Look at well-known books and explore themes and ideas and issues arising. Hold class discussions on the book(s) they are reading.
learning a wider range of poetry by heart	Have a poetry competition. Learn a poem and say it aloud.
preparing poems and plays to read aloud and to perform, showing understanding through intonation, tone and volume so that the meaning is clear to an audience	Have a class assembly on poems they have written on a specific theme/genre. There are four poems in this collection: Autumn (page 32); Cautionary verse (page 34); Silence (page 60) and Song of the Naga (page 66).
understand what they read by:	
checking that the book makes sense to them, discussing their understanding and exploring the meaning of words in context	Use paired or guided reading to ensure understanding. Ask questions to check children's understanding and explain any words that are unclear. The 'Word work' activities encourage children to think about the meaning of words and to look at how they are used in context.
asking questions to improve their understanding	The 'Questions' activities require factual recall and will check pupils' understanding.
drawing inferences such as inferring characters' feelings, thoughts and motives from their actions, and justifying inferences with evidence	Many of the 'Extension work' (EW) activities provide opportunities for drawing inferences from the text. Special examples are: A Bad Business (page 20) – Q7; Daisy Randall … (page 26) – EW2; An Unexpected Visitor (page 29) – EW5; Marley's Place (page 53) – Q6–7; Stately Phantoms (page 71) – EW5; The Case of the Missing Turtle (page 74) – EW4; The Formula (part 1) (page 90) – EW2; Goblin Falls (page 97) – EW3; The School Outing (page 107) – EW2 & 4.

predicting what might happen from details stated and implied	Many of the 'Extension work'(EW) activities provide opportunities for predicting what might happen. Specific examples are: Daisy Randall … (page 26) – EW7; An Unexpected Visitor (page 29) – EW8; Daisy Randall … Continues (page 37) – EW7; The Case of the Missing Turtle (page 74) – EW5; The Formula (part 2) (page 93) – EW3; The Journey (page 100) – EW5.
summarising the main ideas drawn from more than one paragraph, identifying key details that support the main ideas	Provide opportunities for children to chunk text and then scrutinise it carefully to identify key ideas.
identifying how language, structure, and presentation contribute to meaning	Look at different texts to compare and contrast. Pupils should be taught the technical and other terms needed for discussing what they hear and read, such as metaphor, simile, analogy, imagery, style and effect. Some examples from this book include: A Bad Business (page 20) – EW1–3; A Sojourn in Bath (page 23) – EW1–3; Daisy Randall … (page 26) – EW8; Cautionary Verse (page 34) – EW2; Daisy Randall … Continues (page 37) – EW1 & 2; Stately Homes (page 47) – Q8; Snegworthy (page 62) – Q3; Goblin Falls (page 97) – Q7; The Viking Raid (page 111) – EW3.
discuss and evaluate how authors use language, including figurative language, considering the impact on the reader	
distinguish between statements of fact and opinion	
retrieve, record and present information from non-fiction	When using reference books, pupils need to know what information they need to look for before they begin and need to understand the task. They should be shown how to use the contents pages and indexes to locate information. The skills of information retrieval that are taught should be applied, for example, in reading history, geography and science books, and in contexts where pupils are genuinely motivated to find out information, for example, reading information leaflets before a gallery or museum visit or reading a theatre programme or review. Teachers should consider making use of any library services and expertise to support this.
participate in discussions about books that are read to them and those they can read for themselves, building on their own and others' ideas and challenging view courteously	Look at a huge variety of texts to explore the style of writing and understanding. Classes can be broken down into groups to look at specific things and then feed back to the rest of the group.
explain and discuss their understanding of what they have read, including through formal presentations and debates, maintaining a focus on the topic and using notes where necessary	Pupils should have guidance about and feedback on the quality of their explanations and contributions to discussions.
provide reasoned justifications for their views.	

Writing, Speaking and Cross-curricular Activities

Writing, Speaking and Other Literacy Activities	Cross-curricular Activities
A Bad Business, page 20	
❖ Draw up a document listing all Lavinia's assets. ❖ Imagine you are a newspaper reporter. You are about to interview Joseph Grumbleweed. List the questions you will ask him. Then role play the situation with a friend. ❖ Act out the scene where Joseph has to confront Lavinia and tell her about his difficulties. ❖ Imagine that you are a newspaper reporter, write a report on the situation with Joseph Grumbleweed. ❖ Design and make a leaflet for Organics R Us, describing what they do and what their products are. ❖ Design and make a holiday brochure for a holiday in the French Alps.	❖ Draw or paint Lavinia and Joseph Grumbleweed's home. ❖ Lavinia wants you to buy some furniture for her new house in London. Do some research on the Internet and plan how she can spend £50,000 on furniture.
A Sojourn in Bath, page 23	
❖ In play format, write out a conversation between Mrs Armstrong-Ponsonby, Julia's mama and Julia. ❖ Make a 'Wanted' poster for the highwayman. Describe what he looks like and mention the reward. ❖ Act out a scenario where Julia goes to the Pump Rooms to take the waters. She meets the medics who comment on her health, what will they say and what does Julia reply? ❖ Make a small brochure showing the variety of hats on sale at the Milliners. Describe when the hats can be worn and from what they are made. ❖ Design and make a pamphlet giving details of the Bath Waters and how they can restore one's health. ❖ Imagine that you are Fanny and that you are writing to Julia, responding to her letter and describing your news.	❖ Find Bath on a map of Britain. What county is it in? ❖ Find out about the history of Bath. Who built the first town there, and why? ❖ Compare the entertainments available to Julia with those available today.
Daisy Randall and the Victoria Line, page 26	
❖ Imagine that Harry is together with all his cronies discussing Operation Thunderbolt. Act out the discussion and their plans. ❖ Investigate poems written for travellers on the tube. Write a poem of your own for the tube. ❖ Give a report on Operation Bluebird describing what happened – imagine you were actually there at the time.	❖ Look at a map of London and work out where Daisy might live and where she might work. ❖ Daisy's cousin comes to visit. What interesting sights might they visit that are close to Daisy's flat? ❖ Make up a police photofit of Harry the Strangler, using clues given in the passage. ❖ Find out how fast a speedboat can travel. Is that faster than the fastest animal can move?

Writing, Speaking and Other Literacy Activities	Cross-curricular Activities
Daisy Randall and the Victoria Line, page 26 (cont)	
❖ Imagine that you are Daisy, describe the events leading up to Harry the Strangler's death.	❖ Look at a tube map of London and plan Daisy's commute on it. If the journey between stops is about a minute and each stop takes about a minute, work out roughly how long her journey to work takes. Don't forget the walk to and from the tube stations.
An Unexpected Visitor, page 29	
❖ Put the passage into play format and act it out with a friend. ❖ In dialogue form, continue the conversation between Mrs Shah and the tiny person. ❖ Create a tiny person and write a brief biography for them. Choose a name and draw what they look like. ❖ Imagine you are a journalist, write a report for the local newspaper describing the events in Mrs Shah's garden. ❖ The small creature in the garden is not alone! They have plans to make a huge underground city under Mrs Shah's garden. In groups, discuss the benefits of having a new city under the garden for the pixie-like people, produce a report for local residents to say what they will do and how their lives will be changed.	❖ Imagine you are Mrs Shah's next-door neighbour. You see her behaving strangely in her garden, hitting a mound of earth. What do you do? ❖ Design an outfit for the tiny person. ❖ Make a tiny person from linking cubes or card, ^{1}/10th as tall as yourself. ❖ Look at the description of Mrs Shah's garden and do a garden design of it. Draw it to scale and then find the area and the perimeter of the design.
Autumn, page 32	
❖ Find and read some other poems about autumn. ❖ Imagine that you are the mouse – list all the dangers you encounter during the autumn time, describe what you do during autumn. ❖ Research autumn festivals in countries around the world – make a class presentation or assembly showing the different festivals and describing them. ❖ With a partner one of you can take on the role of a farmer and the other a reporter – there has been terrible flooding due to bad weather all over the country, think of some questions to ask the farmer about how he is coping and what this means for him and his livelihood.	❖ Look at information from books and the Internet about how people celebrate harvest. ❖ Find out about the work of various charities and how they help people in developing countries to grow food. ❖ Press some leaves between the pages of a book. When they are dry, use them in a collage.
Cautionary Verse, page 34	
❖ Make a poster showing the verse about Sam, and some 'dos and don'ts' that the reader can learn from it. ❖ Read some of Hillaire Belloc's *Cautionary Tales for Children*. What do you think of them? ❖ Read some more modern cautionary verse. How does it compare to Hillaire Belloc's? ❖ Act out the cautionary verse. ❖ Interview Sam's mother about the situation Write a newspaper report on the incident for the local newspaper.	❖ Choose a cautionary verse you like, and illustrate it.

Writing, Speaking and Other Literacy Activities	Cross-curricular Activities
Cautionary Verse, page 34 (cont)	
❖ Write out a procedure text for helping Sam to stop raiding fridges – discuss this with a friend about what you can do and then list all the things you can do to help Sam – put your results into a clear text.	
Daisy Randall – the Story Continues, page 37	
❖ Read a poem about the river Thames. Or write one. ❖ Do some research about Buckingham Palace, then plan and make a guidebook about the palace. ❖ Imagine you are Harry with his cronies. Devise a conversation you have together about the job you plan to do at Buckingham Palace. ❖ Imagine you are having a telephone conversation with the Queen about the job. Choose whether the Queen is 'in' the job or knows nothing about it. ❖ Write a letter to the Queen explaining the situation. ❖ Harry and his Gang have made a set of instructions for their special 'job'. Write down the instructions clearly in order showing exactly what Harry and his friends plan to do step by step. ❖ Imagine you are Daisy – write a report of the events so far for your boss at MI6.	❖ Look at a map of London and trace a route for Harry from Moorgate station to the river. ❖ Paint a picture, to hang in Buckingham Palace, as part of an exhibition about the Thames.
Feral Cats, page 41	
❖ Make a play of the story and act it out. Make a booklet of all the characters in the story, giving a description of what they look like and what their characteristics are. Use pictures to illustrate your work. ❖ Imagine that you are Shadow – you have to justify your marriage – list all the reasons why marriage will be beneficial for you and for the gang ultimately. ❖ Imagine you are Pancho – write a report about your meeting with White Paws and what was discussed. ❖ Turn the story into play format and continue it. ❖ Research feral cats around the world and make a presentation using PowerPoint for the rest of the class.	❖ Draw a map of the territory where the cats live. ❖ Imagine you are going to adopt a feral cat. Find out how much it costs to feed a cat for a year. ❖ Find out about organisations that help feral cats. Consider whether you or your class might want to support one of these charities.
Game Ranger Diaries, page 44	
❖ Find out more about lions from the Internet and looking at books. ❖ Imagine you are a keeper at a lion or cheetah breeding sanctuary. Detail your day in the form of an itinerary showing what you do each day. ❖ Write an information text about cheetahs.	❖ Paint a lioness with her cubs. ❖ Have a class discussion about hunting big game. Are there occasions when it might be a good thing? Is it always a bad thing? What are your views? ❖ Look at brochures or websites with information about game reserves and use them to plan an imaginary holiday.

Writing, Speaking and Other Literacy Activities	Cross-curricular Activities
Game Ranger Diaries, page 44 (cont)	
❖ Write the conversation between the Grundels when they arrive at the lunch. ❖ Prepare a written itinerary for the Grundels showing all the exciting events and trips planned for them during their stay at the lodge. ❖ Design and make a leaflet or small brochure to advertise the lodge.	❖ Make a brochure of the lodge with details of all the different rooms available and what they are like. ❖ Make a plan of the game reserve showing the various boundaries. Draw the plan to scale and then calculate the area and perimeter of the reserve.
Stately Homes, page 47	
❖ Research birds of prey and decide how to make a presentation on the subject. Will you produce a poster? Give a talk? Create a PowerPoint presentation? ❖ You help to organise events at Woodberry Castle in Scotland. The castle has wooded grounds which surround a large loch. Decide what type of event you are going to have and write a short advert for the magazine, in order to attract visitors. ❖ Imagine you are one of the guides at one of the stately homes and you are giving a guided tour of a couple of the rooms in the house. What will you say about the rooms? Think about your characterisation. ❖ Make a poster for the Actworthy Hall re-enactment of the Battle of River Cresswell. ❖ Design and make a pamphlet to advertise the garden party at Actbridge Manor. ❖ Imagine that you are Denise Walters, the Editor, you have to prepare the next month's issue of Stately Homes, as a class, get into groups to prepare articles for the next issue – be inventive and creative.	❖ Choose one of the activities advertised in the magazine and draw or paint a scene to illustrate it. ❖ Find out from your friends and schoolmates what different kinds of magazines they read, and what they like about them. Consider how to present this information to a newsagent who wants to start stocking a range of magazines for children. ❖ Make a graph (bar or line) showing visitor sales over a period of a few months at a particular stately home. Be creative with your design! How will you boost sales? How will you present your findings to the board?
Enquiry into the Danger Zone at Moon Station Gloid, page 50	
❖ Have a class debate in which half the class provides an argument for closing the Danger Zone down and the other half provides an argument for keeping the Danger Zone open. ❖ Imagine you are doing a commentary on the benefits of the Danger Zone to a small audience of people. What would you say to encourage them to try out the Danger Zone? Act it out with a group of friends taking it in turn to be the commentator. ❖ Imagine you are a reporter talking to Dougal's Mother Henrietta. What questions would you ask her? Try to find out as much as you can in role. ❖ Prepare a report on the enquiry to be put into a newspaper. ❖ List the main findings of the report. ❖ Design a brochure to advertise the Danger Zone.	❖ Think about materials you know (plastic sheeting, wood, cotton fabric, elastic …) and list some properties for each one. Now list some of the properties of reconzirconite, either ones you know from the passage or ones you have invented. ❖ There are seven other areas in the Danger Zone apart from the Black Hole. Imagine you designed one of them. What is it like? What do you have to do in there? What level of difficulty would you grade it as? ❖ Explore what crystals are and how they are made. Draw an Enzolite crystal and say how it is special.

Writing, Speaking and Other Literacy Activities	Cross-curricular Activities
Enquiry into the Danger Zone at Moon Station Gloid, page 50 (cont)	
❖ As a class come up with some conclusions and recommendations and then write them down ready to submit to Gloid.	
Marley's Place, page 53	
❖ Read *A Christmas Carol* by Charles Dickens, and find out about the character called Marley's ghost. That Marley was also a self-made man. You could read the original story or a version specially retold for children. ❖ Marley's House is for sale, imagine you are an estate agent selling it, describe it and its main features, including a picture ready to put in the window of your agency. ❖ Write a dialogue between the people in the house, in play format. ❖ Write a history about the house when it was known as the Gargoyle House.	❖ Paint a picture of the house with the white van in front of it. ❖ Find out about gargoyles and what they were for. ❖ Make a gargoyle from clay.
Obituary: Dame Susan Pettigrew, page 57	
❖ You are going to interview Dame Susan's brother, Jonathan. Make up a list of questions you would like to ask him about their lives as children. Role play the situation with a friend. ❖ Design a brochure or website for a company specialising in luxury tents and equipment for travellers. Describe what makes your tents special. Think about what facilities might appeal to people like Dame Susan. ❖ Write an obituary for any well-known person. ❖ Make up a fictional person and create an obituary for them describing their lives in detail and telling people for what they will be remembered. ❖ Dame Susan, unknown to everyone, kept a diary, write an extract for the day when she rescued the Nepalese woman's grandson.	❖ Look at some patterns on oriental rugs (use books, catalogues or a website). Now design your own oriental rug. You could use squared paper to help you keep the pattern symmetrical. ❖ Roughly when was Dame Susan born? Research what life was like for rich women in those days. How was Dame Susan's life atypical?
Silence, page 60	
❖ Alliteration is an important tool in writing and poetry, if you could amend the poem and add alliteration to it, what would you add and where? ❖ Write a piece of fiction in which you are lost in the woods with a friend and the gloomy shadows are following you – what will happen next? ❖ Rewrite the poem as if it is not winter but summer, think of the language you will use and how it will affect your writing.	❖ Ask a friend to read you the poem while you shut your eyes. Now paint the picture you see when you hear the poem. ❖ Look at some images of snowflakes on the Internet. Describe what they all have in common. ❖ Create a snowflake image of your own. Make it as accurate as you can. What is the angle between the arms? (Remember: turning a whole circle takes you through 360° so the angle between two arms is 1/6 of this.) ❖ Get everybody to stop talking and listen hard. Count the different sounds you can hear.

12

Writing, Speaking and Other Literacy Activities	Cross-curricular Activities
Silence, page 60 (cont)	
	❖ Photograph yourself somewhere special where you are being very quiet and make a class collage using the pictures. Write captions for them showing where you were and what you were doing quietly, eg reading, painting.
Snegworthy, page 62	
❖ Design a poster reminding people to carry their gas masks with them at all times. ❖ Listen to an old recording of the broadcast that told people in England that war had been declared with Germany. With a group of friends make a radio announcement which will be broadcast telling people that war has been declared. What will you say and how will you say it? ❖ Act out the situation on the train from the children's point of view up to the part when they arrive at Snegworthy. ❖ Design a poster to remind everyone about the importance of the blackout. ❖ Write a history of Snegworthy for a guide book. ❖ Write a character profile for Uncle Joe.	❖ Paint a picture of Snegworthy. ❖ Talk with a partner about what you would put in a guest room to make sure the guest felt comfortable and at ease. ❖ Find out what kind of train the children would have travelled on and draw it. ❖ The Second World War lasted from September 1939 to September 1945. How many months did it last?
Song of the Naga, page 66	
❖ Research dragons and collect images of different kinds to make into a poster. ❖ Have a class debate on keeping a dragon for a pet – half the class can be 'for' and half can be 'against'. ❖ Make an information text about the Naga describing what it is like, what it eats, what it likes doing etc. ❖ Make a booklet of dragons – as a class, decide on which aspects you are going to look at and divide the class into groups to work on specific aspects – be imaginative and creative.	❖ Read the poem again, then paint a picture to illustrate it. ❖ Use instruments to create 'the song of the Naga' or some other dragon music. ❖ Use balsa wood to make a dragon skeleton then cover it with a fabric skin. ❖ Make a dragon mask.
Dragon Lore, page 68	
❖ Write a blurb for the back cover of Emerlot's book. ❖ Read *The Lost World* by Arthur Conan Doyle, either in the original or as a simplified version for children. ❖ Make a leaflet showing all the important flora and fauna Thayles can and cannot eat and their nutritional value. Illustrate it showing where these plants may be found. ❖ Make up your version of the Song of the Thayle that the nursemaids might sing to the young dragons in the eggs.	❖ Paint or draw a Thayle. ❖ Find out how to blow eggs. Decorate them and make a dragon's nest for them. ❖ Design a front cover for Emerlot's book.
Stately Phantoms, page 71	
❖ Read *Moonfleet* by John Meade Falkner. It is an exciting story about smugglers.	❖ Draw a map of the area around Toorock Castle.

Writing, Speaking and Other Literacy Activities	Cross-curricular Activities

Stately Phantoms, page 71 (cont)

❖ Imagine that you are a guide at Toorock Castle – describe a ghostly experience of your own, what happened and where did it happen? ❖ Write a play or story in which you describe the events from the smugglers' point of view. ❖ Design and make a leaflet which will encourage visitors to Toorock Castle. ❖ Imagine that you are Iris Delafield – you are giving an account of your visit to Toorock to a reporter, describe the events in your own words to be written down as a report. ❖ Write a play script for the smugglers in which they are landing their cargo – what happens next? Do the excise men get them? ❖ Imagine that you were an eye-witness at the tragic drowning of Penelope Fitzwilliam – describe what happened to be written up as a newspaper report.	❖ Design a dust cover for Griselda's new book. Think about the size of the book and how big the dust wrapper must be to fold around it. Write the 'blurb' for the back of the book and plan what to put on the spine. ❖ Create a visual storyboard to describe the events in the passage to do with either Iris' story or Griselda's experience.

The Case of the Missing Turtle, page 74

❖ Write a speech to give to the rest of the school explaining what your fund raising event is for and why it is important. ❖ Design and make a poster inviting people to come to the village fête. ❖ Write a speech on behalf of the Widows and Orphans Benevolent Fund in which you welcome everyone to the fête, explain what it is for and give details of all the things they can do that afternoon. ❖ You are a police officer investigating the strange disappearance of the turtle and the death of Mr Graves – list the events so far ready to write up into a report for the Chief Inspector. ❖ Miss Wimpole is interested in all the people around her – imagine that you are Miss Wimpole and you have been keeping a character profile on all the villagers, make a small booklet of all your observations – be inventive and creative.	❖ Discuss the work of detectives with your group. What do you know about the job of detective? ❖ Think about any stories you know about detectives. What makes them special or memorable? ❖ Make a turtle out of papier mâché and paint it silver, then decorate it. ❖ If you were organising an event to raise funds for a charity, what charity would you choose? Discuss this question with your group and try to reach a consensus. What type of event would you hold?

The Cookery Competition, page 77

❖ Imagine you are the chief judge. Prepare a little speech to give to all the contestants congratulating them on their hard work and wonderful food. ❖ Find a recipe for something that you like and write it out as a procedure text for your friends. ❖ Research spun sugar and how it is made, then write a procedure text explaining how to make it. ❖ Prepare a speech on the benefits of rice pudding. ❖ Write a profile on Henry Tomkinson.	❖ Discuss with your group what you would choose as a prize for this competition. In what way would the prize be suitable? ❖ Design and make a fancy menu for the judges, listing Denzel's final dishes. ❖ Find a recipe for something you would like to make, and plan how to make it – at home or in school. ❖ Research chef's clothing and draw a picture of Denzel wearing his outfit. ❖ Find out how much it would cost to fit out Denzel in his chef's clothing.

Writing, Speaking and Other Literacy Activities	Cross-curricular Activities
The Cookery Competition, page 77 (cont)	
	❖ Mime being one of the contestants preparing his meal for the competition.
Shopping Centre Opens, page 80	
❖ Divide your group in two. Half of you work together to present a case for having the new shopping complex. The other half of you prepare a case for not having the new shopping complex. Both arguments are to be read out at a meeting of the community in the Town Hall. ❖ Role-play situation: Father Cuthbert is very disappointed about the developments, imagine you are a newspaper reporter and interview him. What questions would you ask? What responses do you think Father Cuthbert would make? ❖ Father Cuthbert has written a letter to the developers – imagine that you are Father Cuthbert, what will you say in your letter to try to persuade them not to build the new supermarket? ❖ List all the reasons why the Portly Street cinema is an asset to the town.	❖ Make a map of the shopping complex so that visitors know where they are going. ❖ In magazines, or on the Internet, find images of new buildings. Survey your classmates to find out how much they like each building. Which is most popular and which least?
The Dark Side, page 83	
❖ A famous story about street children is *Oliver Twist* by Charles Dickens. Read a shortened version of the story (the original is very long). ❖ In play format, write the dialogue that might have taken place between Old Ned and Lucy after he has rescued her. ❖ Look at history books to find out more about beggars. ❖ Continue the story from the point of view of Charlie. What happens to him? Does he find his Aunt? ❖ You are the Underworld King – write a decree in which you explain why you wish everyone to pay regular sums of money to you and what they will get from this in the way of help and protection.	❖ Have a class discussion about how it must feel to be a beggar. ❖ Find out about charities that support homeless people. Consider doing some fund-raising for one of them. ❖ Think about how you could find out whether or not a cardboard box acts as good insulation from cold. Do an experiment to find out. ❖ Describe what you think the Dark Side is and what it wants from Lucy.
Everest, page 87	
❖ Research an aspect of Mount Everest or the Himalayas that interests you and make a short presentation on the topic. ❖ Write and design a leaflet persuading climbers to visit and climb Everest. ❖ Write an article for a newspaper in which you heavily discourage people from climbing Everest – remember to support your argument. ❖ Write your own non-fiction text in which you describe the dangers of high altitude.	❖ Locate Mount Everest on a world map or globe. ❖ Look at a film about climbers who have made it to the top of Everest. ❖ Investigate the 1996 storm and the effect it had on climbers stranded in the Death Zone. ❖ Investigate the mystery of Mallory on Mount Everest.
The Formula (part 1), page 90	
❖ Act out the play with a group of friends. ❖ Continue the play in your own words, what do you think will happen next?	❖ Make a guinea pig puppet. ❖ Find out what country guinea pigs come from and how they live in the wild.

Writing, Speaking and Other Literacy Activities	Cross-curricular Activities
The Formula (part 1), page 90 (cont)	
❖ Add a new character to the play. Describe who they are and how they will contribute to the continuation of the plot. ❖ Imagine that you are the Professor, write out your formula carefully giving detailed instructions about how to make it. ❖ Delilah the Guinea Pig has been asked to give a speech to a medical conference explaining what the formula has done to her and how it has changed her life – imagine that you are Delilah and prepare a speech. ❖ Have a class debate on animals talking and what the future would be like as a result – how might this help/harm the world?	❖ Explore the cost of keeping guinea pigs. How much would it cost per week to keep a pet guinea pig? ❖ Use ICT to make wanted posters of the guinea pigs.
The Formula (part 2), page 93	
❖ Act out the play with a group of friends. ❖ Continue the play, telling what happens next. Don't forget to include the stage directions. ❖ Write character sketches for one or more of the animals. ❖ Write a speech for Professor Patek to give to the board explaining her research and what she has found. ❖ Imagine you are Sam, describe what you do next. ❖ List all the benefits of the formula and all the possible dangers.	❖ Design a stage set for the play, showing the laboratory where the action takes place. ❖ Discuss the importance of research and how animals are sometimes used in this. Discuss the pros and cons of using animals. ❖ If you could choose one of the animals to act which one would it be and why? ❖ Make up some interesting mathematical formula for the experiment. ❖ Draw a detailed floor plan of the laboratory showing where all the cages are. Use area and perimeter to describe how big the areas are.
Goblin Falls, page 97	
❖ In play format, write the conversation between Lord Garth and Ruskin then act it out with a friend. ❖ Continue the story, telling what happens to Lyle and to the Queen. ❖ In play format write what you think the conversation between Lyle and the Goblin Girl will be like. ❖ Write down all the ways in which you would persuade the Goblin Girl to go with you. ❖ Imagine you are Hawkcatcher, write a report in which you justify sending Lyle on such a dangerous mission.	❖ Draw a map of the area and mark all the different places on it. ❖ Make a relationships web showing the different characters and their relationships. ❖ Draw a series of pictures to illustrate the story. ❖ Draw a continuation of this story in cartoon format. ❖ Imagine: how does Lyle get through the Goblin Falls and how does Grace help him?
The Journey, page 100	
❖ Write a poem or a song about a train journey. ❖ Make a booklet of games and puzzles to entertain younger children on a train journey. ❖ Imagine you are the cheerful woman on the train playing cards with Chan, invent a dialogue between them both and turn it into play format. ❖ Imagine you are Luke, describe where you have come from and where you will be going. .	❖ Use an Internet mapping service to find Conwy. If Chan passed through Birmingham to get there, where might she have started her journey? ❖ Use the same mapping service to find out some facts about Conwy, such as where it is near, or what special buildings there are. ❖ Investigate train timetables and journeys. Compare and contrast journey times and prices. ❖ Paint a scene from the point of view of Chan looking out of her carriage window.

Writing, Speaking and Other Literacy Activities	Cross-curricular Activities

The Journey, page 100 (cont)

❖ Prepare a leaflet in which you list and describe the benefits of train travel.

❖ Prepare a travel brochure on Wales – research areas of Wales and then compile a class brochure

The Organisation, page 103

❖ Make a 'Wanted' poster for any of the people in the passage. ❖ Imagine you are Olga. Plan what to do in order to get Mrs Kan to meet The Voice. ❖ The Voice talks about Bonzo Collins. Invent a 'back story' to explain who Bonzo is and his relationship with Mrs Kan. ❖ Imagine that you are the Voice – you have decided to give your workers new code names, what will they be? Prepare a speech to explain the changes you have made and the significance of the new names! ❖ Write a newspaper report on the incident between 'Grandma' and the boys. ❖ Act out the scenario between The Voice and the agents, creating a playscript first.	❖ Draw a plan of the meeting room, showing the table and any equipment you think is there. ❖ Experiment with making a 'secret' video recording through a hole in a carrier bag. ❖ Choose names for the other people around the table.

The School Outing, page 107

❖ Turn the passage into a play and act it out. ❖ Design and print a brochure for the coach company to promote their services. ❖ Research places fairly near your school where you could go for an outing. Work out how you would get there; what time you would leave school and arrive back, and all the costs involved. Write a persuasive letter to your teacher and the head outlining why you should go and explaining what it will cost. ❖ Write a complaint letter to the coach company in which you say how unhappy you are with the service. Detail your complaints carefully. ❖ The head and governors are interviewing for a new teacher. List all the qualities you think a teacher should have. ❖ Continue the story in your own words.	❖ Imagine: at the end of the passage we learn that the coach is bound for Manchester. What does Ella Jenkins do now? ❖ Imagine: Polly and Gary have planned something awful to do on the coach. Describe what happens.

The Viking Raid, page 111

❖ Write a list of daily chores for a Saxon boy or girl. ❖ Do you think Knor should rescue Thyle? Present an argument for or against attempting to rescue her. Imagine you are Thyle. Describe your capture and journey back to the Viking lands. What has life been like for you and the other young slaves? ❖ Continue the story. ❖ Design a brochure for a Viking ship builder illustrating the different boats and describing all their qualities.	❖ Research Viking longboats, then design and make a model longboat. ❖ Design a sail for a Viking longboat. ❖ Find out how fast longboats could travel. How long would it take a longboat to cross the sea to Britain from Scandinavia? ❖ Find out about the kind of huts Saxons lived in, and what they were made from. ❖ Imagine you are one of Raghelm's friends. You do not approve of his plan to rescue Ragsson. Explain why.

Writing, Speaking and Other Literacy Activities	Cross-curricular Activities
The Viking Raid, page 111 (cont)	
❖ Imagine you are a Viking slave – write a diary entry recalling how you were captured and what your previous life was like. ❖ Imagine that you are Thyle meeting Knor again (having just been rescued by him). Write a dialogue for the two of them and then act it out. ❖ Prepare a rousing speech for Filgar to give to his people. ❖ Continue the story. What do you think happens next?	❖ Design an outfit for a Saxon boy or girl. ❖ Imagine you are the wise woman. Describe what you saw in your vision as you looked through the window of the meeting hut and then when you looked at Knor.
The Snagrond, page 115	
❖ You make ships for various adventurers – design and make a brochure showing your various vessels and describing their special features. ❖ Describe what you think will happen next in the story from the point of view of the Snagrond. ❖ Prepare a leaflet for travellers hoping to visit Skullbone Island – describe what it is like, what activities you can do there and what you might see in the way of historical features and wildlife (if any)! ❖ Prepare a leaflet or travel brochure for Turtle Island giving a brief history of the island and its wildlife etc. ❖ Research the kind of ship that Scrawkins might have sailed. Present some information about it on a poster. ❖ Write the invocation for bringing forth the Snagrond.	❖ Draw a map of Skullbone Island. ❖ Paint a picture of Flint, Scrawkins or the Snagrond. ❖ Learn and sing a sea shanty. (What are sea shanties and where does the word come from?) ❖ Imagine you are Scrawkins. Describe how you felt when you saw your old ship, *The Diamond,* burning. ❖ Flint and Scrawkins would have used charts and maps to help them navigate. Sailors often used the stars too. Make a map of the seas around the islands where they sailed showing all the potential dangers they may have encountered and show the stars in the sky which may have guided them. Be inventive with the stars! Give them names too. ❖ Look at angles and distances required in order to fire a cannon ball accurately and hit your target.
Virus on Space Station, page 119	
❖ Design a clear and informative poster which tells people what symptoms to look for and what to do if they have these symptoms. ❖ Role play: one person is Doctor Jasmine Wetherby and the other is a radio reporter who is interviewing her about her theory. ❖ Design a fabulous new leaflet all about the wonderful Sigfelm Delta Colony. ❖ You are the Minister for Health – you have been asked to prepare a speech to deliver to the inhabitants of TwoPluto Rhumba and other space stations in the area informing them of events about the disease so far. You need to be very informative, you also need to give advice and explain what evacuation procedures might have to take place. ❖ Write a newspaper report of your own on the events so far on the space station.	❖ Design a space shuttle for travelling between Space Station TwoPluto Rhumba and Earth. ❖ If the disease was deliberately introduced to the holiday resort, describe how you think it might have been transported there. ❖ Design and make a shuttle timetable giving information about all the departure and arrival times to TwoPluto Rhumba and how much flights cost. Will there be different prices for economy and business class?

Writing, Speaking and Other Literacy Activities	Cross-curricular Activities
Virus on Space Station, page 119 (cont)	
❖ Write a biography about the small boy in hospital. ❖ As a fiction text, describe what will happen next in the story.	

A Bad Business

Joseph Grumbleweed grimaced. It was a bad business. A very bad business indeed. He swallowed hard.

'Is it all lost?' he asked hoarsely. William Carstairs nodded gravely. Joseph's wrinkled face went white. 'Everything … even the shares in Tumbleweed Industrial?' Carstairs nodded again. In all the forty years Carstairs had worked for him, Joseph Grumbleweed had never seen him make a mistake like this.

Joseph slumped miserably in his thick, leather chair. 'Then I'm done for,' he mumbled weakly. 'Ruined … utterly ruined. What on earth will Lavinia say?'

At the mention of Joseph's wife, William Carstairs flinched. A wave of pity for Joseph washed over him. It would take a strong man to face the wrath of Lavinia Grumbleweed.

A sick feeling gripped Joseph. He had gambled the family home on this deal. Everything … even Lavinia's prized horses. How could he possibly tell her it had gone?

'You'll have to tell her,' he whispered.

William paled. 'I, sir?'

'Yes, you William. You tell her. She likes you. She'll kill me if I do it.'

Carstairs was horrified. 'She'll kill you if you don't,' he spluttered. 'You can't let her find out from me. She would never forgive you!'

The phone rang abruptly. Both men jumped.

Joseph was tempted to let it ring. Deep inside him an idea was forming. A one-way ticket to somewhere hot, tropical and obscure beckoned. A quiet place, where no one would find him. Then he came out of his dream. Shakily, he stretched out his hand and picked up the receiver.

It was Lavinia. She knew.

Lavinia's wrath whipped through the family home like a tornado. Her prized horses were her greatest joy. Heartbroken she had watched them all being boxed into horse trailers and taken away. Now rage filled her as she surveyed the fields, idle and empty without their usual occupants. Joseph had done this. His greed had reduced them to this pitiful state and deprived her of the creatures she loved best. Her face, blotched and tear-stained with grief, hardened suddenly. She picked up the telephone and punched in the

Brilliant Activities for Reading Comprehension, Year 6

© Charlotte Makhlouf and Brilliant Publications Limited

numbers. At last a woman's voice answered it.

'Henry Mead, please,' snapped Lavinia. A blast of classical music filled the earpiece while she was put on hold. Moments later, her financial advisor was at the other end of the line.

'Henry Mead speaking.'

'Henry, it's Lavinia Grumbleweed. I need to talk to you.' Briefly she told Henry Mead, everything that had happened. Henry said nothing and then he laughed. The laugh took Lavinia completely by surprise.

'I don't find the situation amusing at all,' she said frostily. 'This morning I watched my horses being taken away. In a few weeks I will have to leave my home, the home I have lived in and cherished for the past twenty five years, and you just laugh.'

'But my dear Lavinia,' said Henry consolingly, 'surely you cannot have forgotten your own money, your shares, and your properties up in the French Alps?'

Lavinia Grumbleweed banged down a fist onto a mahogany table inlaid with mother-of-pearl. 'Of course I haven't forgotten my own money,' she almost shouted down the phone. 'It's all gone down the drain, thanks to Joseph. I put everything into Joseph's ridiculous little scheme and now I've lost it all!'

Henry smiled. 'Not quite everything, Lavinia. I must apologise, but I'm afraid I rather misled you as to where I had invested your money. I disobeyed your orders and didn't invest in Tumbleweed Industrial as you told me to.'

There was a stunned silence at the other end of the phone. Then Henry Mead heard Lavinia's voice, shaky and uncertain. 'What property in the French Alps? Have I property up there?'

'The property you bought twelve years ago. That building has now trebled in value. Two new chairlifts and a large new cable car have been built nearby, and the village is now a highly desirable ski resort.'

'And my money … where did you put my money, Henry?'

'A very successful company called Organics R Us. You're a rich woman, Lavinia.'

'Then I can get my horses back?'

'You can get them back and buy some more horses if you want,' Henry chuckled.

Lavinia sat down heavily, still clutching the phone. Henry Mead had been in charge of her personal fortune for almost thirty years and this was the first time he had ever gone against her wishes. It took a strong man to flout Lavinia Grumbleweed. But now gratitude and relief flooded through her.

'How dare you disobey my wishes, Henry,' she growled down the phone, 'But I'm deeply grateful to you for doing so.'

Questions

Answer the following questions with a full sentence:

1. What bad thing has happened to Joseph Grumbleweed?

2. What caused this problem?

3. Joseph is fearful of his wife's response. Why is this?

4. What do you learn about the character of Henry Mead from the passage?

5. How has Henry saved Lavinia's fortune?

6. Why has Lavinia's property in the French Alps 'trebled in value'?

7. What do you think prompted Henry to go against Lavinia's wishes?

Word work

1. Give the meaning of the following words:

   obscure

   flinched

   blotched

   mahogany

   wrath

2. What is the role of a financial advisor?

Extension work

1. Find an example of a simile. How well does it convey meaning?

2. Give an example of how the writer conveys tension in the early paragraphs.

3. Identify two sentences which you feel are particularly striking and the effect they have on you as the reader.

4. Identify two sentences which describe Lavinia's bad mood.

5. If you were Joseph, how would you break the news of his great losses to Lavinia? What would you say?

6. What do you think of Lavinia's character?

7. If you were very rich, like Lavinia, how would you spend your money? How would you spend your time?

A Sojourn in Bath

My Dearest Fanny,

We are come to Bath at last! Mama is much relieved, for the journey has been a trial to her. Having no male protector has given her the vapours and I have not been able to leave her alone for the shortest moment. Indeed she would not even suffer the coachman near her for fear he would take advantage of her, poor man – though a dear, kind-hearted soul he turned out to be. He watched over us with great assiduity and we had cause to be exceedingly grateful to him for one of our fellow travellers proved to be a common criminal! He slipped away from the Blue Boar Inn without paying for his room.

I wish you were here, dear Fanny, for it looks as if we shall have a good few months of excitement and entertainment. We are comfortable with Aunt Alice and Uncle Stephen who have a most spacious residence in Lansdown Crescent. Aunt and Uncle are delighted to have us and Auntie is already planning card parties, luncheons and picnics for us. Every day will be filled with some event.

We have a beautiful view of Bath and the surrounding gardens, which has quite restored Mama's health already, and she has been willing to walk into town or take a sedan chair to visit friends and the library. We have heard a number of recitals at the Pump Rooms and tried the spring waters there, which Mama professed to be 'quite vile'.

You would not credit how many people come to drink the Bath waters. The number is quite astounding. They see physicians who examine them and find the most curious ailments imaginable. Even I, whose health is most robust, am considered to be quite jaundiced, and told to take a course of treatments. Mama and I have made no further journeys to the Pump Room to take the waters but have spent our time walking along the canal and becoming acquainted with the shops.

Outside Mrs Adams' millinery shop we met Mrs Armstrong-Ponsonby. Both Mama and I were shocked at how stout she has become since we saw her in London. She had three small, white dogs with her, all of whom wore adorable blue and pink bows. Mrs Armstrong-Ponsonby was delighted to see us and confessed in hushed tones that she has over-indulged herself on pastries, and has come to Bath in order to take the waters on the advice of her doctor. I profess that I do not share her doctor's faith that the waters will reduce Mrs A-P's ample figure. But she is determined to take her treatments and swears she will not succumb to the town's many culinary delights.

Mrs A-P has been in Bath for two weeks already, and was able to enlighten us on a number of interesting events. Apparently Mr Erskine Adams is in town. He is one of the most eligible catches a young lady could wish for. He has in excess of fifty thousand pounds! Mrs A-P informed us that the young ladies present at the Pump Rooms the other evening were in a twitter at his arrival and could hardly be restrained from introducing themselves. Mama was shocked at such unladylike behaviour and I received one of her lectures on what is considered appropriate.

Oh, but I nearly forgot. We met Lady Sally Stevenson yesterday. It would appear that her journey to Bath was fraught with danger. Her carriage was stopped by a highwayman, who robbed her of all her jewels. Had her driver's pistols not jammed in the firing he would have shot the fellow. Lady Sally said she was sure she has seen the highwayman before, his bearing was familiar. But I cannot see how a lowly highwayman would be familiar to her. The reward for catching him is three hundred guineas.

I have to confess that I should like to meet this highwayman, whoever he might be. He sounds most romantic and dashing. I would be intrigued to know where he hides his person. There must be some tavern where he spends his time. You must promise not to tell Mama that I have written this, for she has already told me what she thinks of men who rob unprotected ladies on the highway.

Uncle Stephen's gout is giving him much pain at the present time. His doctor has advised tepid baths filled with lemon juice to ease the agony but I cannot see Uncle Stephen doing what the doctor orders. He had a huge plateful of prawns cooked in white wine last night which Mama thinks made the attack worse, but you know what Uncle Stephen is like when it comes to food. He consults with his chef, Antonio, on a daily basis, to plan the menus each evening and the richness of the meals must be seen to be believed. There was so much on the table last night it would have fed thirty people, not just the four of us.

I confess I felt slightly uncomfortable at the waste for there were no fewer than eight courses and a choice of five puddings. When I think of those poor ragged urchins in the streets, just skin and bones, it fills me with guilt. I will speak with the housekeeper and see if Signor Antonio might be prevailed upon to give the leftovers to those needy children.

Promise me, Fanny dearest, that you will heed the doctor and take your medicine regularly and that you will never go out unless you are well wrapped up. The wind is terrible at this time of year and what might seem like a gentle breeze may become the strongest of gales.

Dearest Fanny, I will write to you again as soon as I have more news. Until then I send my greatest love to you and everyone at The Elms.

Your most devoted sister,

Julia

Questions

Answer the following questions with a full sentence:

1. What relationship is the writer of the letter to the recipient?

2. What complaint does Uncle Stephen suffer from?

3. What do you learn about Uncle Stephen's character from the passage?

4. What do you learn about Julia's character from the passage?

5. How does Julia feel about the highwayman who robbed Lady Sally Stevenson?

6. What different entertainments are available to Julia and her mother in Bath?

7. Why is Mr Erskine Adams so popular?

Extension work

1. Describe how and why the writer uses a distinct style of language for the passage.

2. Identify two sentences which you think are particularly striking, and the effect they have upon you as the reader.

3. How do we know that this letter was not written today? Use *five* examples from the passage to support your argument.

4. Describe two ways in which food is an issue in the passage.

5. Imagine: why has Julia's sister Fanny not come to Bath with them?

6. If you were with Julia in Bath, which entertainment would appeal to you the most and why?

7. Imagine you are the highwayman. Describe the incident with Lady Sally Stevenson from your point of view.

8. Imagine you are one of Mrs Armstong-Ponsonby's dogs. Describe your typical day.

Word work

1. Give the meaning of the following words:

   coachman
   urchin
   highwayman
   milliner
   eligible

2. What do you think *'the vapours'* might be?

Daisy Randall and the Victoria Line

Daisy Randall had not always worked in a bank. There had been a time when she worked as a secret agent for MI6. That was eighteen years ago when she had been fitter and slimmer. Now she had exchanged intrigue and danger for a quieter life, one that was calm and predictable and considerably less dangerous, an office life in which each day was the same: same routine, same people, same work. Daisy had thought she would miss the excitement and the danger but she had not. It was good to know that each day she would get up at exactly the same time, catch the tube to her office, and at precisely 5:30pm each evening she would leave the office and return to Victoria, where her flat, her sister Doris and an evening meal awaited her.

This morning she caught the tube from Victoria as usual. It was packed with hot, flustered people. Daisy clung to a strap as the train jerked abruptly forwards. She bumped against a stout woman who lost her footing and bounced against a tall young man beside her. No one said 'sorry'. They just accepted that these were the hazards of public transport. Daisy shut her eyes and tried to pretend she was not jammed like a sardine between so many other people.

Soon the train came to a screeching halt and the doors opened. More people crammed themselves in. Daisy wished she had walked to work through the park. She was too old to be squashed against all these bodies, fighting for air. Thankfully she only had another two stops to go. The tube lurched into motion once more and Daisy looked up. She saw a man stare briefly at her and then turn away. Daisy froze.

That face! It couldn't be! Harry the Strangler!

Daisy gripped the strap even more tightly. Her heart was pounding inside her chest.

Harry the Strangler! What on earth was he doing here? Daisy turned nonchalantly and

Brilliant Activities for Reading Comprehension, Year 6
© Charlotte Makhlouf and Brilliant Publications Limited

gave the man a brief glance. The man seemed to have no idea he was under scrutiny. He was staring out of the window with hard, mean eyes. Daisy had seen those eyes before, she could swear it. She had seen them looking at her, above the barrel of a gun he was pointing at her. There was a small scar in the man's hairline. Harry the Strangler had a scar like that.

Daisy turned away and swallowed hard. It couldn't be Harry the Strangler, because she, Daisy Randall, had killed him twenty-one years ago.

The tube lurched wildly and Daisy took the a chance of another furtive look at the man with the scar. He looked just as dirty and badly dressed as Harry had been.

But it couldn't be Harry! Harry had been killed in Operation Thunderbolt with three of his cronies. Killed by Daisy herself on the choppy waters of the Mediterranean.

Her mind went back twenty-one years. She could remember Operation Thunderbolt as clearly as if it had taken place yesterday. The assignment had involved several shady individuals and some beautiful diamonds. The diamonds had been restored to their rightful owners but only after a number of people had lost their lives at the hands of Harry the Strangler. There had been a shoot-out from the back of a speedboat when Daisy had finally put an end to Harry.

Or had she?

Now Daisy wasn't so sure. She cast her mind back. She remembered shooting Harry quite clearly. She could still see his body tumbling off the speedboat into the water. But even though they had searched, they had never found his body, for the current had done its work and washed him away. The body had simply vanished.

Daisy shut her eyes.

Perhaps Harry the Strangler had survived. Perhaps he had only been wounded and had managed to struggle to safety. 'Maybe I didn't kill him,' thought Daisy. She gripped her briefcase tightly, her brain working swiftly.

She could just get off the train at her stop and forget she had ever seen Harry. Go to work and get on with her job and no one would be any the wiser – unless Harry got up to his old tricks again. Or she could follow him and see where he went and what he was up to.

The tube slowed as it approached Daisy's station. The doors beeped loudly and then opened. A flood of people gushed off the train and made their way to the exit.

Daisy got off with them, her heart beating wildly. She took a few steps down to the next carriage and stopped beside the open doors. The 'exit' sign beckoned. She could follow it to the escalator, which would take her up to the street …

The doors began beeping. Instinct and her MI6 training kicked in.

A dangerous man was on the loose. Daisy leapt through the tube doors just as they began to close … .

Questions

Answer the following questions with a full sentence:

1. Does Daisy regret giving up her job as secret agent?
2. What does Daisy enjoy about her present life?
3. In what way is travelling by public transport considered hazardous?
4. Why does Daisy think that the man on the train cannot be Harry the Strangler?
5. What clues suggest to Daisy that it might be Harry the Strangler?
6. What temptation does Daisy face towards the end of the passage?
7. How does she deal with this temptation?
8. Which phrase or phrases tell you Daisy has made a decision about what to do next?

Word work

Give the meaning of the following words:

lurched

flustered

scar

intrigue

nonchalantly

assignment

Extension work

1. Explain what you think the role of a secret agent is.

2. Why do you think Daisy remembers Operation Thunderbolt so well?

3. At the end of the passage, do you think Daisy makes the right decision? Give reasons for your answer.

4. Imagine: who did the diamonds belong to and how were they stolen?

5. Another dangerous mission Daisy went on was Operation Bluebird. Describe what Daisy did in this operation and whether or not it was successful.

6. Write about Harry's experience during and after the speedboat chase. How did he escape?

7. Continue the story. What happens next to Daisy?

8. How does the writer try to convey Daisy's sense of anxiety when she thinks she sees Harry?

An Unexpected Visitor

At the bottom of Mrs Shah's garden the small mound of earth had increased in size. Mrs Shah focussed her binoculars and watched. Every so often the mound would push upwards like a miniature volcano then small clusters of earth would trickle down the sides. It was most peculiar.

She had noticed the mound earlier that morning. Shuffling down to the bottom of the garden to check on her tomatoes, she had seen that her patch of emerald green lawn was spoiled by a small patch of earth. At first she had thought it was moles but on closer inspection she realised that no self-respecting mole could inflict such precise damage. Moles, reflected Mrs Shah, were haphazard when it came to digging. Their holes varied in size and the quantity of soil displaced. This particular mound was of a particular neatness and it kept on growing.

Mrs Shah returned to the house to perform a few necessary chores. Every so often she picked up her binoculars and monitored the mound of earth. She could see a definite increase in the amount of earth spilling out over the lawn.

By mid-morning she had had enough. Stomping down the garden path in her Wellington boots, she picked up a large spade from beside the potting shed. If it *was* a mole wrecking her lawn, then it would soon have the biggest headache she could give it! As she stood over the mound she realised that it had almost trebled in size. Annoyance coursed through her. It had taken years to get the garden looking beautiful – years of pruning, clipping, feeding, weeding – and now some creature was ruining her lawn. She hefted the spade with all the strength her frail arms could muster and brought it down heavily on the mound of earth. Under the earth there was a sharp clang and a tiny voice squeaked 'ouch!' Mrs Shah stepped backwards in shock, her arms tingling. The spade had connected with something made of metal and the shock waves reverberated up her arms. Surely something had spoken too. She stood stock still, her mouth a wide 'O' of dismay.

In front of her, the mound moved and jerked. A large pile of earth swooped upwards and then toppled over the sides of the hole in a crumbled mess. Mrs Shah lifted the spade once more and, without thinking, brought it down heavily on the mound. Again there was a squeak of alarm and then a small figure scrambled up and out of the hole, coughing and spluttering in annoyance. Mrs Shah stepped backwards. Something small, green and strangely human-looking was glaring at her furiously and shaking a tiny fist.

'What are you trying to do?' shouted the small figure in a shrill voice. 'Are you trying to kill me?'

Mrs Shah opened her mouth in astonishment and then closed it again. She rubbed her eyes carefully and stared at the figure. It was definitely a person. A very tiny person, but still a person, and the tiny person was livid with rage. Its sharp, pixie-like face was contorted with fury and its hands were bunched into fists. Mrs Shah could not be sure what it was wearing because it was liberally smeared in earth, but she thought she could make out a jerkin and shorts under the thick coating of mud and grass.

'Well?' snapped the tiny figure, shaking its fist up at Mrs Shah. 'Are you trying to kill me?'

Mrs Shah looked around carefully then rubbed her eyes again. She removed her glasses slowly, checked the lenses then replaced them on her nose. Perhaps her medication was making her unwell. She should go to the doctor for a check-up. She peered once more at the tiny figure, bending her creaky knees to get a closer look.

A clod of earth struck her full in the face. Mrs Shah straightened up and frowned. Now she knew she was not seeing things. 'Who are you and what are you doing in my garden?' she asked sternly.

Brilliant Activities for Reading Comprehension, Year 6
© Charlotte Makhlouf and Brilliant Publications Limited

Questions

Answer the following questions with a full sentence:

1. Why is Mrs Shah looking through her binoculars?

2. Why does Mrs Shah dismiss the idea of it being moles that have made the mound on her lawn?

3. To what is the mound likened?

4. How do we know that her garden is important to Mrs Shah?

5. Name some of the garden jobs that Mrs Shah does to make the garden beautiful.

6. Give three clues that tell us that Mrs Shah is not a young woman.

7. Why is it difficult to see what the creature is wearing?

Word work

Give the meaning of the following words:

miniature

monitored

trebled

frail

jerkin

Extension work

1. Choose six adjectives from the passage which you think enhance the description of characters or events.

2. At the beginning of the passage, what did you think the mound might have been?

3. Is the tiny person's response to Mrs Shah what you expect? Say why.

4. Do you think Mrs Shah is justified in her actions?

5. What do we learn about Mrs Shah's character from the passage?

6. Do you think the characters of the tiny creature and Mrs Shah are alike in any way? If so, how?

7. What do you think the little figure has been doing under the garden, and why?

8. Continue the story. What do you think will happen next?

Autumn

The dying leaves fall from the trees

And rest their weary selves upon the barren land.

There is a coldness to the air, a sparkling crispness

That heralds the onset of winter's coming glory.

Our fingers search for conkers,

Scuttling through the blanket of leaves,

The trees' former glory.

Delighted, we find the hard shapes and show them,

Resplendent in their shining coats of brown.

We are blessed with Nature's bounty.

As the fields relinquish their might

And prepare us for the months ahead.

The storehouse fills to the rafters, where

Eager mice wait.

We see fruits of the harvest upon our tables

And remember those who work to

Nourish and sustain us.

Then we give thanks for the blessed rain

And warming sun, without whose presence

Their labours would be nought.

Autumn is here again.

Brilliant Activities for Reading Comprehension, Year 6

© Charlotte Makhlouf and Brilliant Publications Limited

Questions

Answer the following questions with a full sentence:

1. How do we know this passage is about autumn? Give three examples from the poem.

2. Do you think that the poet likes autumn? Why do you think that?

3. Why are the mice eager?

4. What do you think the fruits of the harvest might be?

5. Autumn's arrival is a celebration. Do you agree? Use the passage to help justify your response.

6. What themes do you think the poem touches upon? Justify your response with examples from the poem.

7. What do you think the poet means by the line 'winter's coming glory'?

Word work

1. Give the meaning of the following words:

   heralds

   resplendent

   barren

   sustain

2. '*... the fields relinquish their might ...*' What do you think is meant by this?

Extension work

1. Which time of the year do you think is most special? Say why you think that.

2. Write a poem about your favourite season.

3. Which part of this poem do you like best? Give reasons for your answer.

4. The poet mentions a mouse. What other animals do you think the poet could have used in writing about autumn?

5. Write another verse to the poem in which you introduce another animal.

6. Imagine you are one of the mice in the poem. You are being interviewed by a newspaper on getting through the winter. Describe the difficulties you face and how you manage to survive.

7. Comment on the style of the poem and the language used. How effectively do you think it has been used?

Cautionary Verse

There was a boy whose name was Sam.

He was so awfully fond of ham.

He'd raid the fridge whenever able

And guzzle ham beneath the table.

He ate some ham for lunch and tea;

He even ate it secretly,

In the garden, in his room,

In the cupboard with the broom.

His mother soon became annoyed.

With diverse punishments she toyed

To try to teach her naughty Sam

Not to raid the fridge for ham.

Now it happened that one day

Sam had gone to a friend to stay,

And feeling peckish late that night

Sneaked to the kitchen by torchlight.

The fridge was stuffed with yummy treats:

Pastries, pies and sticky sweets,

Little tarts, a chocolate cake.

How his friend's mum loved to bake!

Sam's greedy eyes began to beam

At this simply luscious scene.

Then to his complete delight

He spotted a most glorious sight:

A leg of ham, both thick and crumbly.

His greedy tummy felt quite rumbly.

Without a single 'by-your-leave',

Out came the ham in one quick heave.

Brilliant Activities for Reading Comprehension, Year 6
© Charlotte Makhlouf and Brilliant Publications Limited

The awful boy began to eat
That whole joint of tender meat.
He scoffed it down in simply seconds.
A tasty meal, our Sam did reckon.
Then to his horror he began to swell.
He really did feel most unwell,
And staggering miserably to his feet,
He beat a sickly, green retreat.

In the morning, I am sad to say
Sam had simply passed away.
His fondness for large cuts of ham
Quite finished off poor greedy Sam!

When told of her poor son's demise
Tears sprang to his fond mother's eyes.
So hearken children; listen dears,
Raiding fridges ends in tears!

Questions

Answer the following questions with a full sentence:

1. In which places did Sam eat?

2. What do we learn about Sam's character from the verse?

3. At the house of Sam's friend, who enjoyed baking?

4. Find some words that make it clear that Sam did not ask for a snack at his friend's house, but helped himself.

5. What is the moral of this verse?

6. How do we know that Sam has gone too far with his eating?

7. Look at the structure of the verse and discuss in your own words how it is managed.

Word work

1. Give the meaning of the following words:

   raid
   diverse
   luscious
   scoffed
   demise

2. What is a *'cautionary'* verse?

3. *'He beat a sickly, green retreat.'* What do you think is meant by this line?

Extension work

1. Give this poem a title. What would you call it and why?

2. Does every pair of lines rhyme? Do you think all of the rhymes work well or are there some that don't sound right to you?

3. Which part of the poem do you like best and why?

4. What do you think Sam's parents could have done to stop his bad habit?

5. Try writing an alternative ending for this verse.

6. Try writing a piece of cautionary verse of your own. Think of some behaviour to warn children about, then think of something that might happen to a person who persists in doing it.

7. Humour is an essential part of cautionary verse. Why do you think this might be so?

Daisy Randall – The Story Continues

Daisy had been thinking about Operation Thunderbolt when the tube train ground to an abrupt halt. She looked out onto the platform and saw that Harry the Strangler had left the train. This was the moment she had been waiting for. She and Harry had unfinished business to settle. Daisy pushed her way through the throng of people, and flung herself out onto the platform. Ahead of her, Harry was making his way casually up the escalators. Daisy followed him discreetly. A voice inside her head warned her that she was being rash; that she should contact one of her friends still working at MI6 and let them know what was going on. But she ignored the voice. She had a score to settle with Harry the Strangler and it had to be settled her way!

At the top of the stairs, Daisy felt a moment of panic as she realised Harry had vanished. Then she caught a glimpse of him standing by a newsstand. As she watched Harry buy a packet of sweets and the *Racing Times*, Daisy pretended to look at a carousel of postcards. Then she followed Harry as he left the station. Her training as a secret agent flooded back; she used the crowds for cover and assumed a nonchalance she did not feel.

Up on the street Harry quickened his pace. Moorgate was not an area Daisy knew well but clearly Harry did. She followed him through a maze of streets until ahead of them she saw the river Thames. Was Harry making for the river? He had got ahead of her now and Daisy almost ran down the road in her desperation to catch up with him. Suddenly a hand reached out and grabbed her by the neck. The attack took Daisy completely by surprise. She felt herself being jerked backwards by a powerful arm, then she was wrenched around to face her attacker. It was Harry the Strangler.

'You're following me!' snarled Harry, giving her a vicious shake. 'Why?'

The hands around Daisy's throat tightened and she gasped for air. 'You've been following me for quite a while now,' hissed Harry, his face pressed close to Daisy's. 'Since the station in

fact. Now, why's that, I wonder?'

Daisy winced. Not only were Harry's hands choking her, his foul breath was making her feel ill. Unable to stand it any longer, Daisy lashed out with her briefcase. It slammed viciously into Harry's right kneecap, and he released his grip on Daisy's throat. Daisy followed up with a couple of slick, crisp moves that had Harry on his knees on the pavement groaning in agony. Daisy dragged him to a small corner where they would be hidden from passers-by and slammed him up against the wall.

'Hello, Harry,' she said, quietly.

Harry's eyes widened in horror as he recognised his opponent. 'Oh lawd. It's you, isn't it?'

Daisy stared at him without compassion. It was the same old Harry, but older and more grizzled. He had acquired another scar, which pulled one corner of his mouth upwards and snaked across his left cheek.

'I thought you were dead,' said Daisy, her eyes never leaving Harry's face. Harry scowled and tried to wriggle free. The pressure on his arms increased and he winced with pain.

'Let me go,' he snarled, 'I've done nothing wrong!'

Daisy raised an eyebrow. 'That's difficult to believe,' she said smoothly, 'when you've spent most of your life harming people. Tell me, Harry, what's a nasty man like you doing in a nice place like London?'

Harry grimaced and shut his mouth tightly, but his eyes shifted furtively to the river. Daisy smiled. So Harry had a boat waiting down by the river. No surprises there. Her brain worked swiftly. The main problem was that she had no weapon, so she needed support. She applied careful pressure to Harry's neck and watched him slump to the ground motionless. Daisy

flexed her fingers. It was an old trick, useful in times of emergency; the victim would be out cold for about fifteen minutes, which would give her a breathing space. Keeping her eyes fixed on Harry she took out her mobile phone and punched in a number. It was a number she had used many times in the past. She had never forgotten it.

'It's Randall here. I need backup,' she told the person at the other end of the line, knowing that her phone call would provide her exact location to those who needed it. She could hear the confusion at the other end of the line, the whispered voices, the consultations. Then someone else picked up the phone.

'Randall,' barked a voice. 'What the devil's going on? How dare you use this line?' It was Colonel Savage, Head of Operations.

'It's Operation Thunderbolt,' Daisy began. The voice down the phone inhaled sharply. 'I have Harry the Strangler here and I need backup.' She could hear the flurry of activity in the background.

'Are you sure?' snapped the Colonel.

'Absolutely. He was on a train headed to Moorgate. I recognised and followed him. At present he's out cold but I need help quickly.'

'Williams will be with you shortly,' said Colonel Savage. 'Keep Harry there … and don't do anything risky.'

Daisy snapped her mobile shut and opened her briefcase. She took out a roll of brown parcel tape and set about taping up Harry's arms and legs. A minute later, Harry groaned weakly and his eyes fluttered open. Then a look of pure hatred crossed his face and he tried to sit up. Daisy dragged him upright and shoved him against the wall.

'So Harry, why are you so anxious to get to the river?'

Harry pursed his lips together. 'I'm on a job.'

Brilliant Activities for Reading Comprehension, Year 6

© Charlotte Makhlouf and Brilliant Publications Limited

He almost spat out the words.

'Of course you're on a job, Harry,' sneered Daisy, 'I want to know what job.'

'They'll kill me if I tell you!'

'And I shall kill you if you don't. The job, Harry, what is it?'

'Burglary.' Harry's eyes slid away from Daisy's.

'Perhaps you could be more specific, Harry.' Daisy raised her hand warningly.

'Buckingham Palace,' he replied quickly. Daisy said nothing. Harry was lying, of course. How on earth would he and his cronies burgle Buckingham Palace? The security was so tight, they stood no chance. The idea was absurd. Daisy burst out laughing.

'So you think it's funny!' Harry snarled. 'We'll wipe the smile from your face, you wait and see. The Queen will have nothing left by the time we've finished. Not a single painting or piece of silver. She'll have to cancel all the guided tours because there won't be anything for the public and tourists to see.'

Daisy wiped her eyes with a handkerchief. 'It's not foolproof, you idiot,' she snapped. 'It's the most ridiculous plan I have ever heard of. Why you'd never even get through the gates. "Oh, excuse me, officer,"' mimicked Daisy in a mincing voice, '"but my friends and I have come to rob the Queen. Do you mind if we bring our vans through and park in front of the main entrance?"' Daisy burst into laughter again as Harry's face turned ashen.

'It is foolproof,' he said in a hoarse whisper. 'We're going to use the sewers and ship out all the stuff via the Thames. It's a brilliant plan, cunning and brilliant, and the Queen's going to help us shift the stuff. I've spoken to her and she said she would.'

Questions

Answer the following questions with a full sentence:

1. Where does the story start?
2. Why is Daisy following Harry?
3. Has Harry changed since Daisy last saw him? If so, how?
4. What is the 'job' Harry is planning?
5. What role will the river Thames play in the job?
6. When Daisy learns about the job what is her reaction?
7. What do we learn about Harry's character from the passage?
8. What do we learn about Daisy's character from the passage?
9. '*How dare you use this line!*' What is the Colonel angry about ?

Word work

1. Give the meaning of the following words:

   abrupt
   throng
   nonchalance
   winced
   flurry
   cronies

2. If you are '*without compassion*' what does this mean?

3. If something is '*foolproof*' what does this mean?

Extension work

1. Why do you think the writer predominantly uses dialogue within the passage?
2. Comment on the different types of sentence the writer uses to convey mood.
3. How does Daisy cope with the challenges of her situation, given that she is no longer a secret agent?
4. If you were Daisy, and had seen Harry on a tube train, what would you have done? Why?
5. Write character profiles for Harry and Daisy.
6. What do you make of Harry's claim that the Queen is going to help him rob the palace? Explain why he might have said that to Daisy.
7. Continue the story and write what happens next.

Brilliant Activities for Reading Comprehension, Year 6
© Charlotte Makhlouf and Brilliant Publications Limited

Feral Cats

There was a moon that night. Juniper and I were out hunting when Dino stopped us. He was the black cat who lived at the Italian restaurant on Broad Street. He was sitting on a fence behind the restaurant, looking uneasy.

'Pancho's crossed the line,' he told us softly, his green eyes wary. Beside me I could feel the hackles on Juniper's neck rising.

'Are you sure?' I asked, my heart beating more swiftly.

Dino nodded. 'One-Eye saw him going over the allotments and down to the children's playground. He crossed the line and went into the Fangs territory about an hour ago.'

Juniper's eyes met mine. Crossing the line into another pack's territory was dangerous. The different packs were always careful to hunt within their own territory. Moving out of that territory could lead to fights or worse.

'Why did he do that, Patch?' Juniper's voice trembled. 'He knows the rules.'

I shrugged. 'Come on, we'd best get back to Shadow.'

Shadow was the Claws leader. She was a huge silver tabby, more like a tiger than a cat. No one knew where she had come from. There were rumours that she had left the comfort of her human home and traded it for the freedom of the wild. One wet, stormy night, she just turned up in the Claws territory. Shadow refused to say where she had come from. She took our oath and became a member of the pack, and within a few months she'd become our leader. The best we've ever had. She'd been leader for over two years now.

In those two years, Shadow had kept the peace with the other packs, even the dreaded Fangs. Shadow had a gift, the ability to read the thoughts of others and respond accordingly.

'Peace is a gift,' she often said. 'We must work to protect it.'

Now, tonight, that peace was at risk, all because of Pancho.

Juniper and I raced back to the crumbling outhouse where we lived, by St Cuthbert's Church. It was a good place, peaceful, protected and it had a patch of green grass where we could lie in the sun or play. Our pack was not a big one, but we had quite a few youngsters and the garden area was great for them.

Moth Ear was on sentry duty at the gate when we streaked around the corner. Her face looked puzzled as we flashed past her over the mass of overgrown grass. The outhouse was part stone and part wood. There was no door, and the

roof had lost a few tiles, but inside it was warm and fairly dry. The other cats were there now, curled up sleeping amongst old rags and pieces of disused carpet. Some of the youngsters were playing. They stopped when they saw us and looked up.

'Pancho's crossed the line into Fangs territory.'

Everyone sat up, alert and watchful.

'Are you sure?' asked Scar curtly.

Juniper and I nodded.

Scar hissed softly under his breath. 'Fool!' he snarled. 'If it comes to war it will be because of his stupidity. Why did he do it?'

'Because I told him to,' said a soft voice.

In a dark corner of the outhouse two glowing amber eyes flashed in the darkness. There was silence and I could feel my fur standing on end. Every cat looked tense and alert. From out of the darkness, Shadow padded slowly. The moonlight glinted on her perfect stripes and her muscles rippled. She was almost twice the size of any other animal there. Her face was calm and unruffled.

Scar glared at her. 'You have put us all in danger,' he snarled furiously. We all knew that Scar longed to be leader and to usurp Shadow's power.

Shadow's eyes narrowed to mere slits and she looked at the younger cat.

'Calm yourself, Scar,' began Shadow, her voice controlled and authoritative. 'Pancho is my emissary. I have sent him to negotiate.'

Scar looked openly hostile now and two of his cronies jumped down off the beams and slunk to his side. The whole pack was gathered by now, waiting and watchful. Even the youngsters had stopped their playful antics.

'Negotiate what?' Scar was scornful.

'My marriage.' Silence enveloped the pack. I could hardly believe my ears. What talk was this? The Claws did not unite with other packs. They chose their mates from within and thus the safety of the pack was assured.

'But the law amongst us is quite clear,' I began tentatively. 'We do not marry outside our clan.'

'Laws can be changed,' replied Shadow, her face an imperceptible mask. 'If the Claws are to stay strong we need new blood in the clan. It is time to put aside foolish differences and start building alliances, rather than creating barriers.'

An elderly ginger tom, with a ragged tail, limped forwards. 'Shadow is right,' he said firmly. 'We need new blood to give us strength. But have you considered what might happen to Pancho as your emissary? White Paws will surely kill him.'

'Thank you for your support, Half Tail.' Shadow smiled briefly at the elderly cat. 'You need not worry about Pancho. His safety is assured.'

'You are very certain about his safety, Shadow!' hissed Curled Whisker, flicking her tail unpleasantly from side to side.

'I am,' replied Shadow. Her eyes burned deeply into Curled Whisker's without flinching. 'Why should a brother kill a brother?'

There was silence in the outhouse. Not a cat stirred.

Eventually Half Tail growled out, 'Did I hear correctly?'

Shadow nodded. 'You did … and so did the rest of you. Pancho is White Paw's brother.'

'But why has he never said anything?' Curled Whisker looked shocked.

'Every cat has a right to his own secrets,' replied Shadow smoothly. 'Pancho had reasons for his. When he returns, he might tell you them.'

Brilliant Activities for Reading Comprehension, Year 6
© Charlotte Makhlouf and Brilliant Publications Limited

Questions

Answer the following questions with a full sentence:

1. Who is telling the story?

2. Why are Juniper and Patch concerned when they hear that Pancho has '*crossed the line*'?

3. What gift does Shadow possess? What makes it important?

4. Why is Scar aggressive towards Shadow?

5. Who is White Paws?

6. Who has sent Pancho to White Paws and for what purpose?

7. Why does Shadow think that White Paws will not kill Pancho?

8. How do we know that the cats are sleeping rough? Give two examples from the text.

Word work

1. Give the meaning of the following words:

   wary

   territory

   usurp

2. What is a '*feral cat*'?

3. Scar says, '*If it comes to war it will be because of his stupidity.*' Explain what he means.

4. Pancho has gone as '*an emissary*' for Shadow. What is the job of an emissary?

Extension work

1. Choose two sentences which you feel are very significant to the story and explain why you chose them.

2. Why do you think Shadow might have left the comfort of her home to become feral?

3. Which cat do you feel the most sympathy for and why?

4. Who do you think are the most important characters in the story? Explain why.

5. Do you think Pancho should have kept his relationship with White Paws a secret?

6. Write the conversation between Pancho and White Paws when they meet.

7. Write a character profile for one of the cats.

8. Continue the story.

Game Ranger Diaries

Sunday 1st July

Where have the Wokitap lions gone? Marian and I fear a pride takeover for we saw the bodies of a number of very young cubs near their last sleeping place. The jackals and vultures had not yet got to them so we could tell which cubs they were. We were bitterly disappointed as the cubs had been introduced to the pride only a few months ago and were doing well.

Our trackers Pani and Shosha have been going around the reserve all night in a desperate attempt to find the rest of the pride. They spotted two large males near the edge of the reserve. Pani says he has not seen them before and thinks they have crossed into our land from the Kruger National Park. The larger of the two was injured. He was licking a nasty gash on his shoulder which indicates there was a fight. There is still no sign of Ramu, our pride male. Marian says she will spend the rest of the day searching with Pani and Shosha. I must stay at the Lodge. Mr Lewis is arriving in a couple of days to hunt the old eland bull and I need to ensure everything is ready for his arrival.

LATER

Marian has radioed through to say that Akira and her cubs are safe and well on the small island. We are both relieved to hear this. I was terribly afraid she had brought her cubs out to introduce them to the rest of the pride, but clearly she feels they are still too young to meet the others. This is excellent news. Let's hope she keeps them hidden. Marian told me she was very nervous and wary and when she heard the jeep she took the cubs into dense grass. The water around the island is drying up, but there is enough there to make it a good sanctuary for the moment.

No sign of Ramu.

Monday 2nd July

The lodge is very nearly full. We have some new American guests called the Grundels. They are very keen to see lions and elephants. Bud and Norma Grundel own a chain of diners in Colorado. They had so much luggage with them, it took two porters to carry it. They've booked one of the new suites. We're very proud of them because they're furnished to an extremely high standard and each suite has a viewing platform over the reserve, and a private dip pool. There are six of these suites and already four of them have been taken. The Grundels were keen to get going into the bush, so Adam, one of our other rangers, took them out in the jeep.

Marian has just radioed in to say she has found Ramu.

Friday 6th July

A busy few days. Ramu is sick. He has appalling injuries from a fight with the other males.

Marian and Pani found him lying wedged between some rocks at Leopard Gorge. He is very, very weak. Our vet, Dingane, went out to see him a few days ago. He said it looked bad, but he didn't want to interfere unless he had to. He prefers to let nature take its course. Ramu was weaker by Wednesday morning so Dingane decided to dart him and treat his injuries as best he could. Dingane had no difficulty darting the old lion; he was so sick he barely moved from his spot amongst the rocks. We all worked to help him, setting up a rough operating table. Dingane swabbed and stitched the gashes on his hind legs. I was shocked at how deep they were. Infection was already setting in so Dingane gave Ramu an injection of antibiotics.

Pani has been keeping watch over Ramu since the operation. The lion is still weak but he is showing signs of some recovery. We all hope for the best but there is still no sign of the other cubs and females and it is clear the older males have been driven away from the pride.

Saturday 7th July

Mr Lewis arrived this morning. He is a large, brisk man who seems used to giving orders. He owns a printing company in England. He brought a couple of hunting rifles with him, which look very new. I wonder if Mr Lewis has done much shooting. Thankfully he had brought all the necessary licences with him. Our last hunter forgot his licences so that he was not able to hunt.

Ralph and I took Mr Lewis out to the hunting camp. The camp is situated a few miles away from the main lodge in a different area from where the tourists go. Ralph usually acts as guide. Today I could see him eyeing up Mr Lewis sceptically. He was keen to get Mr Lewis over to the rifle range as quickly as possible to see how well he could shoot. Mr Lewis scowled deeply but allowed himself to be taken there. Ralph kept him a good hour while I busied myself checking the equipment. Afterwards Ralph pulled me aside. 'I'm not taking him out,' he said flatly.

I was aghast. 'Why not?'

'He's a menace! Didn't have a clue how to load the gun and can't shoot straight. I'm not risking him killing one of us.'

'But he's come all this way. He can't go back, he's paid for this trip.'

Ralph's face clouded over stormily. 'I'm not having him wounding that animal and causing it suffering. Are you going to break the news to him or shall I?'

Ralph is right. We can't have inept hunters on the land. They can cause serious injury or death. But Mr Lewis has paid for the privilege of being here and I can hardly tell him to go home. We must find an alternative solution.

Ramu is improving slowly, but he looks very thin and frail.

Sunday 8th July

Pani and Shosha have found the Wokitaps.

They crossed back from the Kruger late last night into our reserve. We could see that some of the females had been injured as a result of that awful fight. Pani counted only six cubs instead of the usual thirteen. Only one of the young males was with them. Pani said they were all very nervous. They could hear the other two males roaring not far away. It is clear that Ramu has done his best to safeguard the pride, but unless he recovers sufficiently, the pride will be taken from him very swiftly.

Questions

Answer the following questions with a full sentence:

1. Who do you think is writing the diary?

2. Why do you think the writer is disappointed at the death of the cubs?

3. What do you think is meant by 'a pride takeover'?

4. What tells you that the lions mean a lot to the person writing the diary?

5. Between Monday 2nd July and Friday 6th July there are no diary entries. Why do you think this might be?

6. Why is Mr Lewis visiting the reserve?

7. What concerns does Ralph have with Mr Lewis?

8. What improvements have been added to the lodge to make it special for visitors?

Extension work

1. Which day's diary entry do you find the most interesting? Give reasons for your answer.

2. 'Ralph is right. We can't have inept hunters on the land. They can cause serious injury or death. But Mr Lewis has paid for the privilege of being here and I can hardly tell him to go home. We must find an alternative solution.' What do you think the writer and Ralph should do?

3. What do you think will happen to the Wokitap pride of lions?

4. Write a diary entry for Monday 9th July describing what happens next.

5. Imagine you are Marian and you have just found Ramu. Describe what you see and what has happened.

6. You are Mr Lewis. Write a letter or email home telling about your experiences so far at the reserve, and what you expect will happen to you next.

Word work

1. Give the meaning of the following words:

    inept
    gash
    dense
    sanctuary

2. Dingane, the vet, is keen to 'let nature take its course'. What do you think is meant by this?

Stately Homes

Monthly Magazine   June issue

DEAR READERS,

IT HAS BEEN an exciting year for us here at **Stately Homes** and I'm delighted to announce that our magazine is flourishing. This month, we report on some exciting new developments at Bagnum Hall as the restoration of the Great Hall and Library get underway. A team of experts are using their considerable talents to recreate the beauty of a bygone age. The costs of the restoration, which are likely to be five million pounds, are to be defrayed by the Bagnum Hall Trust, supported by generous donations from private individuals.

In this issue we celebrate Spirits Month. This is an opportunity for all those interested in ghosts to find out more about the spirits which haunt many ancient homes. It will also give our staff the chance to gather information for a new book, **Stately Phantoms**, to be published next year. If you have had an encounter with a phantom, please get in touch with Griselda Hall, who will be delighted to hear about your experience. Her email address can be found at the back of the magazine.

One topic we report on this month is badgers. The keeper at Griddlecote Manor has reported a rise in the number of badger setts to be found around the Manor. This has led to much damage to the garden, and the main lawn has been returfed for the fourth time this year. In a controversial article, Mary Baxter proposes new ways for keeping the badger population under control. If you have any views on this subject do please let us know.

For those readers with children, don't forget to look at our new activities page at the rear of the magazine. A comprehensive guide gives you all the latest on fun-packed activities for children of all ages.

We look forward to a happy, colourful month.

Denise Walters
Editor

Activities Around the Country

THEXTON HALL

HOME of the Lidwyddle Family.

Saturday 7th July

Medieval Jousting Day Children are invited to come and design shields and swords in the arts and crafts tent.

Mr Clive Heston will be bringing his collection of goshawks, sparrow-hawks, falcons, kestrels and owls to the Hall. Clive will give a talk on the history of falconry and show his birds in a display. Children over the age of five will be given the opportunity to handle the birds.

COSGROVE MANOR

Saturday 14th July

Tree planting ceremony

An old vegetable garden has been dug over and is to become an orchard.

Come and assist the gardeners in planting 100 new apple and pear trees.

ACTWORTHY HALL

Saturday 14th July

Recreation of the Battle of River Cresswell

Visitors are invited to join this mock battle which commemorates the time when Lord Reginald Actworthy led his servants and peasants against his neighbour, Bernard de Courtney, who he accused of stealing his sheep. The battle took place mostly in the River Cresswell. Please bring a change of clothes. Non-swimmers are advised to stay away.

ACTBRIDGE MANOR

Friday 27th July

Garden Party

Tickets cost £8 for non-members and £6 for members.

Concessions for children are available.

Tickets to the greenhouse are on a first-come-first-served basis and cost £6.

The garden party is an annual event and gives visitors the opportunity to explore the beautiful gardens which are only open a few times during the year.

BODDLEWORTHY CASTLE

Friday 27th July

Archery Show

While the adults shoot their arrows, would-be Robin Hoods are invited to join the fancy-dress parade. There will be prizes for the best costumes. During the afternoon there will be a barbecue. Please contact Mary Richards at Boddleworthy Castle for tickets.

Brilliant Activities for Reading Comprehension, Year 6

© Charlotte Makhlouf and Brilliant Publications Limited

Questions

Answer the following questions with a full sentence:

1. How many times a year does the *Stately Homes* magazine come out?

2. What is a 'stately home'?

3. Who or what is paying for the restoration work on Bagnum Hall?

4. Name two of the topics which are dealt with in this month's issue.

5. Why do you think that Mary Baxter's article on badgers is likely to be controversial?

6. Who was Lord Reginald Actworthy and what action is he remembered for?

7. Why do you think tickets for the greenhouse are on a '*first come, first served*' basis?

8. Comment on the style of language used for the magazine.

Word work

1. Give the meaning of the following words:

    bygone
    haunt
    encounter
    comprehensive
    falconry

2. Bagnum Hall is being '*restored*'. What does this mean?

3. What will people expect to see at the joust?

4. How do '*concessions*' benefit people?

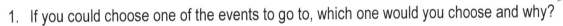

Extension work

1. If you could choose one of the events to go to, which one would you choose and why?

2. What kind of person do you think *Stately Homes* might appeal to?

3. Write an email to Griselda Hall in which you describe a ghostly experience you have had. Say where and when it happened and provide as many details as you can.

4. You are one of the phantoms at Bagnum Hall. What changes have you experienced over the years and how do you feel about these?

5. Write a letter to the editor of *Stately Homes* in which you object to children being allowed into stately homes. Give reasons to support your argument.

6. As editor, respond to the above.

Enquiry into the Danger Zone at Moon Station Gloid

EARTH DAY: APRIL 18TH 3019
(50TH MOON CYCLE)

UNDERTAKEN BY JUDGE WETHERBECK

The enquiry was set up in order to look at the activities within the Danger Zone, in response to a fatal accident which happened in one section of the zone, namely the Black Hole.

OVERVIEW OF THE DANGER ZONE

The Danger Zone was conceived and designed by Dr Marcia Evans, an engineer with enormous experience. Assistance came from many sources, including Dr Beryl Tandy, Professor Joseph Green, Professor Michael Tochs, The Institute for Developing Science, The Human Body Research Station at Vectra Quadrant, Space-Technics Ltd, and Dr Kiel of Space Age Developments.

The idea behind the Danger Zone is to provide a series of challenges for individuals looking for thrilling adventures within a reasonably safe environment. The zone is divided into eight sections, which vary in difficulty. Entry is on the following terms:

- Only people aged 18 and above are allowed to enter the zone

- People entering the zone do so at their own risk and sign a disclaimer showing that they understand what they are undertaking

- If people get into difficulties they will be assisted out of the section, provided there is no danger to staff

- People with injuries are attended to by medical staff who are trained to a high standard.

SAFETY PROCEDURES

Regular checks are made to ensure that:

- all structures are safe

- staff are fit and healthy

- all first-aid stations are up-to-date and fully equipped

- all screening paperwork is accurate.

The structures of the Danger Zone are checked weekly by maintenance crews. Should any section be considered unsafe, it is immediately closed. Repair work is carried out immediately and all details of this are logged. A section is not re-opened until it has been passed as safe by qualified technicians.

THE BLACK HOLE SECTION

The Black Hole is the most dangerous and challenging of the eight sections in the Danger Zone. It is isolated from other sections to minimise any danger from the suction known as the 'Black Hole Effect'.

There are specific entry criteria:

- People wishing to enter must first undergo a series of rigorous training sessions to ensure that they are adequately prepared

- Individuals have to show that they are strong physically and are able to withstand intense pressure and extreme climbing conditions

- If staff feel that the Black Hole is beyond

Brilliant Activities for Reading Comprehension, Year 6
© Charlotte Makhlouf and Brilliant Publications Limited

the capabilities of an individual they refuse admittance and, in fact, very few people enter this section.

The structure of the Black Hole is made from a special fabric called reconzirconite whose special properties allow it to withstand intense pressure and suction and ensure that other areas within the Danger Zone are not affected by the pulling power of the Black Hole.

The 'Black Hole Effect' is created by a machine which generates a vast amount of suction or pull, simulating the pulling effects of a real black hole. If an individual is dragged into this, they are pulled down a large helical tube which leads out to space. Once a person enters the hole, there is no chance of them being rescued.

The challenge in this section is to cross the black hole by means of a solitary rope-haul bridge high above the hole. An additional thrill is the chance that this might be the day when an Enzolite crystal, worth millions of zircons, appears hovering in the air above the bridge for anyone to take.

Once on the bridge, a person must continue as there is no way back. Anyone lacking the stamina to cross the bridge drops directly into the hole. There are no safety nets under the bridge because the pulling force of the hole would rip them to shreds. Should a person get into difficulties on the bridge, their only chance of rescue is a large grabbing device which can grip them and pull them off the bridge to safety.

THE ACCIDENT

Dougal Brown entered the Black Hole section of the Danger Zone in the afternoon of March 30th at around 2:00pm. In his preliminary fitness examination, he was considered to be of higher than normal strength and of excellent physical fitness. He had no physical disabilities

and his records show that he had no specific health issues. The certificate from his doctor pronounced him sound in body and mind. Dougal gave his age as being 18 years old. His mother, Henrietta Brown, has since confirmed that he had just had his eighteenth birthday.

By the time he entered the Black Hole, he had already been in four of the other sections already. People are recommended to take the challenge of the Black Hole early in the day while they have enough energy.

Staff at the Black Hole said that he did not appear tired when he entered the zone. 'He was laughing and joking with his friends,' said Marietta Jones, one of the members of duty staff. 'He said he hoped that he might be the person to collect the Enzolite crystal and make his fortune.'

Dougal was halfway across the bridge when he lost his grip on the rope. Staff quickly noticed that he was in difficulties and tried to catch him with the grabbing device but they failed and he fell into the suction machine.

CONCLUSIONS AND RECOMMENDATIONS
(to be discussed)

Questions

Answer the following questions with a full sentence:

1. Why was the enquiry set up?

2. Which particular section of the Danger Zone is being looked into?

3. Who designed the Danger Zone?

4. What is the purpose of the Danger Zone?

5. Which is the most dangerous section in the Danger Zone?

6. What might happen to a person if they get into difficulties in the Black Hole section?

7. Describe what a person must do, and what they must avoid, in the Black Hole section.

8. How do we know that Dougal was not considered to be tired when he entered the Black Hole?

9. What information do we have that Dougal may actually have been tired after all?

10. How could the rope-haul bridge present a problem?

Extension work

1. Do you find the idea of the Danger Zone appealing? Give reasons for your response.

2. In your own words, describe how the Black Hole effect is created.

3. Why do you think the report has been divided into sections with headings?

4. What recommendations would you come up with to improve the safety of the Black Hole section?

5. You are one of Dougal's friends who was with him in the Danger Zone. You have been asked to give a statement on Dougal's condition when he entered the Black Hole area. Make a detailed statement which will be included in the report.

6. Write the conclusions and recommendations you feel are necessary for the Danger Zone.

7. Write an article for a newspaper in which you strongly condemn the Danger Zone. Give reasons for your views.

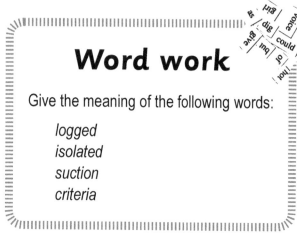

Word work

Give the meaning of the following words:

logged
isolated
suction
criteria

Marley's Place

Marley's place stood shrouded in an early morning mist. Wispy drifts hung like wraiths on the still, cold air. Birdsong filled the neighbouring wood, joyous and sweet, a cacophony of different sounds blending effortlessly into harmonious accord.

The place was known as the Gargoyle House by locals, who loathed the ugly lumps of carved stone which jutted out beneath the roof. The creatures' gloating eyes and open mouths leered down on one and all.

'I'm a self-made man,' Marley had boasted to all who cared to listen. 'I'll put what I like on these here walls.' But in the end Marley had left the house. He said the quiet depressed him. Now the Gargoyle House lay empty and unwanted and the wilderness had begun to encroach, clothing the lawn, and then the house walls, with creepers, brambles and other greenery.

At the edge of the garden, three children watched the house, ignoring the dawn chorus and the lifting mist. The land around them steamed gently as the soft rays of a rising sun kissed the earth awake.

'Imogen, do you recognise it?' hissed the tallest of the children. In front of the front door was a white van. It was devoid of markings or advertisements. Even the number plate was obscured by thick mud.

Imogen bit her lip in puzzlement and shook her dark, curly head. 'It's no one I know,' she whispered back softly, 'and I know all the vans in the village. That one comes from somewhere else. What do you think, Sniffy?'

Sniffy rubbed his nose with the back of his sleeve. His grimy face looked blank and unsure. 'Don't know! Never seen it.'

'How are we going to get in, Jack?' Imogen looked worried.

Jack's intent face stared at the house. Marley's place had been their special den. For months they had been able to come and go as they pleased. Now, if someone was going to move in to the house, they would be forced to find another hideout.

'Do you think the place has been sold?' asked Sniffy. 'Perhaps they're builders and they've come to check on things.'

Imogen shook her head vehemently. 'Don't be daft, Sniffy! Builders have stuff written all over their vans to tell people who they are. This van has nothing. Even the number plate's covered with mud. I reckon they don't want people to know who they are. What do you think Jack?'

Jack turned and eyed Imogen speculatively. 'I think you might be right, Imogen. I think we need to investigate things a little further.'

'What's "investigate", Jack?'

'It means to find out more, you clot, that's what!'

'Look out!' Imogen ducked into a clump of shrubs, 'there's someone at the window.' The other children scurried for cover. Standing at one of the windows on the ground floor was a rough looking man. Peeping cautiously out, Jack could see him looking out towards the weed-filled gravel drive. Another man joined him. Jack's heart began to thud unpleasantly. The second man looked familiar for some reason, but he could not place him. Both men turned abruptly.

'Must be someone calling them,' thought Jack. 'That means there could be three or more of them.' There was a tug at his sleeve. Sniffy was looking up at him with worried eyes.

'Let's go, Jack,' he mouthed, edging backwards slightly and wincing as a thorn ripped at his cheek.

'We can't go, Sniffy. We have to get the stuff from the attic. We'll sneak in,

get the stuff and then creep out again. They'll not see us if we go the secret way.' Two pairs of nervous eyes looked at him.

'I think we should wait until they've gone,' said Imogen, glancing at the window. The two men had vanished from view and the house was silent.

'I think we should get out while we can,' said Sniffy. 'I've got a bad feeling about all this.'

'But we can't leave our stuff,' persisted Jack. 'Those men will take all our things and we've worked hard for it all. I don't want to lose my share, do you?' He saw doubt and indecision in his friends' faces.

'Jack's right,' began Imogen reluctantly. 'We worked hard for that stuff, we don't want to lose it now. I reckon we can sneak up the back way and get out before they even notice us.'

'Let's go then,' urged Jack, 'before we change our minds. Come on, Sniffy, it'll be OK.'

The three children crept stealthily towards the back of the house. The back door

Brilliant Activities for Reading Comprehension, Year 6
© Charlotte Makhlouf and Brilliant Publications Limited

was unlocked, as they had left it last time. It opened smoothly. Jack was glad he had taken the precaution months ago of oiling the hinges and lock. Inside the back door was a small wooden staircase.

The children knew every corner of the house. They made their way stealthily up the stairs, avoiding the creaking steps, until they came to a narrow corridor which opened out into a wide landing. From the landing a wide staircase descended in a gracious curve towards the hall and the front door. Cautiously they peered down. From the room by the front door came voices, raised in anger. An argument was going on.

Jack crept forwards. The voices interested him. What were these people doing in an abandoned house, arguing? He felt a tug on the back of his jacket. Imogen's white face pleaded with him to move away from the staircase.

'Come away,' she mouthed.

There was a sudden crash from below, a sharp yelp of pain, and sounds of a scuffle. The three children froze.

Two figures burst out of the downstairs room, flung open the front door and bolted outside. A vehicle's engine fired into life and the sound of tyres churning up gravel could be heard. Then there was silence.

For a while the children remained hunched together, unmoving and silent. Then at last Jack spoke.

'Shall we go down and find out what's happened?'

Questions

Answer the following questions with a full sentence:

1. Who did the house once belong to and why did the owner leave?

2. Why is the place known as Gargoyle House?

3. How many children are there in this story and what are their names?

4. What have the children been using the house for?

5. Why are the children reluctant to enter the house today?

6. Which of the children seems to be the leader? Give reasons for your answer.

7. What do you learn about Sniffy's personality from the passage?

8. Why is Jack keen to go into the house?

9. Why are the others reluctant to support him?

Word work

1. Give the meaning of the following words:

   shrouded
   obscured
   encroach
   cacophony
   vehemently
   cautiously

Word work (continued)

2. The van was *'devoid of markings or advertisements'*. What does this mean?

3. What is meant by the expression '*a self-made man*'?

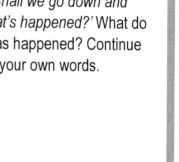

Extension work

1. How does the mood of the opening paragraph contrast with the rest of the passage? Why do you think the writer might have wanted to make this contrast?

2. Write your own description of early morning, based on where you live. What can you hear? What can you see?

3. What *'stuff'* do you think the children have hidden in the attic?

4. Write a character profile for one of the children.

5. Invent a reason why the people with the van are in the house.

6. Jack asks '*Shall we go down and find out what's happened?*' What do *you* think has happened? Continue the story in your own words.

Obituary: Dame Susan Pettigrew

DAME SUSAN PETTIGREW, who has just died aged 96, was one of the world's great experts on rugs. Her passion began when she was a child. The family home was filled with an assortment of beautiful rugs which her family had collected from all over the world. Her Father, the great traveller Reginald Pettigrew, went to many countries, bringing back an enormous collection of wool and silk rugs of varying sizes and patterns, one of which was given to him from the tent of Sheik Omar bin Nuldeen.

When only 20, Dame Susan wrote a book entitled *History of the Rug*, which she based on this unique collection. The book includes many photographs from her family's collection of rugs.

Dame Susan herself knew how lucky she was to do just what she wanted with her life. Her mother had made a small fortune which, on her death, was divided equally between Dame Susan and her brother Jonathan. The money enabled Dame Susan to travel and spend time doing what she loved most: investigating and collecting rugs.

To many, Dame Susan was an eccentric individual. When she travelled, she spurned hotel accommodation, and preferred to stay in her own large tent, which was decorated internally with no fewer than forty rugs.

Dame Susan often said that every rug had a story to tell. Her most prized rug was given her by an elderly Nepalese woman. The rug had taken years for the elderly woman to make and had cost her her eyesight. Dame Susan had rescued the woman's grandson from drowning in a fast-flowing river and the rug was given in thanks. The pattern on the rug describes the daily life of the family. Dame Susan said this was what she cherished most about the rug.

Dame Susan's second book, *Rugs of the World*, provides a fascinating insight into methods of rug-making. We are transported to parts of the world where rugs are still made by hand, as well as informed about factory processes. In *Rugs of the World*, Dame Susan pays tribute to the thousands of women around the world who support their families by making rugs. Dame Susan has set up a small community in Nepal where women make and sell rugs, and the profits are ploughed back into the community for the good of all. The project has allowed women to use their skills to take their families out of poverty. Tourists visit the community and purchase the rugs, which are fairly priced.

Dame Susan was childless, and her will specifies that her entire collection be left untouched at her home in Derbyshire. The rugs will be on display throughout the year. Trustees have been appointed to oversee the management of her house and collection.

Dame Susan brought glamour to the world of Oriental rugs. Because she spoke eight languages fluently, she was able to communicate with thousands of people and learn their stories as told through their rugs. 'She made me feel that the world was my oyster,' reminisces Gabriel Dwight. 'The world will seem a drearier place without her.'

Dame Susan Pettigrew spoke only last week to a rug conference in Delhi, saying: 'I will always be grateful to my parents for allowing me the freedom to live my own life, in my own way, at a time when most women's lives were constrained and dull. I have watched the sun go down from the outside of a Bedouin tent and galloped over the Sahara sands. I have trekked through the Patagonian plains and haggled my way through the bazaars of Istanbul. I am eternally grateful for a life I have enjoyed to the full.'

Now the sun has gone down on a deeply charismatic individual who will be sorely missed.

Brilliant Activities for Reading Comprehension, Year 6

© Charlotte Makhlouf and Brilliant Publications Limited

Questions

Answer the following questions with a full sentence:

1. What is an obituary?

2. What enabled Dame Susan to spend most of her time travelling and collecting rugs?

3. In what ways can Dame Susan be considered eccentric?

4. What did Dame Susan do to help people in Nepal?

5. What was Dame Susan's second book called and what was it about?

6. In what way do you think women's lives were 'constrained and dull'?

7. What do you learn about Dame Susan's parents from the passage?

Word work

1. Give the meaning of the following words:

   eccentric
   spurned
   cherished
   pay tribute
   constrained
   charismatic

2. What does *'I felt as though the world was my oyster'* mean?

Extension work

1. From what you have read about Dame Susan, which achievement do you think is her greatest and why?

2. *'Her entire collection* [will] *be left untouched at her home in Derbyshire. The rugs will be on display throughout the year.'* Imagine you are Dame Susan. Explain why you have put this in your will.

3. For Dame Susan, many of her rugs had a story to tell. Imagine you have found a rug. Describe where you found it and what makes it so special.

4. Imagine you are Dame Susan. Write about one of your adventures as you travelled the world. Think about what you might have been doing, the location, the people you met, etc.

5. *'Now the sun has gone down on a deeply charismatic individual who will be sorely missed.'* What do you think this means and do you agree with the statement?

6. In her book Dame Susan *'pays tribute'* to the thousands of women in rug making. Why do you think she does this?

Silence

Silence.

The night falls

And the sigh of the wind

Fades.

Watch,

In the darkening woods,

As gloomy shadows melt into

Tangled undergrowth.

Listen,

As the faint rustle

Of pattering feet

Lessens.

The warm sanctuary of home is found.

Silence.

The patterned flakes

Drift lazily,

Blanket the ground.

The cold seeps into

Our weary bones

And numbs our senses.

Will we find our way?

The white wasteland

Confuses us and the

Tangled branches clutch at us.

Does the wind call our names?

Listen.

Silence.

Questions

Answer the following questions with a full sentence:

1. Where does the poem take place?

2. In the first stanza, what time of day is the poet writing about? How do we know this?

3. Describe what you think the poem is about.

4. The poem is called Silence. But what sounds are mentioned in the poem?

5. Who or what do you think the 'gloomy shadows' could be and why do you think they 'melt into tangled undergrowth'?

6. To whom do you think the 'pattering feet' belong?

Word work

1. Give the meaning of the following words:

   pattering
   sanctuary
   seeps

2. What is meant by 'white wasteland'?

Extension work

1. Do you think Silence is a good name for the poem? Why?

2. If you were asked to give this poem another name, what would you call it and why?

3. Which of the two stanzas appeals to you the most and why?

4. Extend the poem by writing a verse of your own.

5. Choose a single word which appeals to you and write a poem around it.

6. Describe being lost in the snow. Do you find your way home?

7. Write a story about someone or something that lives in the woods.

Snegworthy

Mother sent us to Snegworthy when the first bombs began falling.

'You'll be safe with Uncle Joe,' she told us, the lines on her forehead creasing with worry. 'I'll feel happier knowing you are in the country away from all this.' She gestured towards what was left of the houses opposite. There had been a particularly vicious air raid last night by the Germans. Their bombs had missed our house but the ones opposite took a direct hit.

'I shall miss you all desperately,' Mother said, fighting back her tears, 'but I can't risk you staying here.'

Mother telephoned Uncle Joe to let him know we were coming. We could hear her pleading down the telephone; he didn't want anyone to stay, let alone three young children. We never knew how she persuaded him, but the following day she sent us off on the first available train to Scotland.

Uncle Joe was Mother's older brother. He lived alone in an old farmhouse in Scotland called Snegworthy. Lionel,

Cynthia and I had never met our Uncle Joe. Mother always spoke of him a bit nervously. Uncle Joe had never married and, in the few photographs we had seen, he looked unsmiling and unfriendly.

'You will behave yourselves,' she told us, hugging us fiercely at the station. 'Do as your uncle says and try not to get into trouble. Anne, I'm putting you in charge, as you're the eldest.' She fussed around us, checking our bags and gas masks, as the tears streamed unashamedly down her face.

'I love you all,' she whispered, embracing us once more. 'Remember not to eat all your food at once,' she warned. 'It has to last you until Scotland!'

Finally, the whistle blew, the flag was

Brilliant Activities for Reading Comprehension, Year 6

© Charlotte Makhlouf and Brilliant Publications Limited

waved and the train began to chug slowly out of the station. We crammed our heads out of the window, waving frantically at Mother, until she was out of sight. Cynthia began to cry.

'I don't want to go,' she sobbed desperately. 'Why can't Mother come with us?'

Lionel hugged her gently. 'She can't Cynth. It's because she loves us so much that she's sending us away. Shall we play a game?'

Our journey was long and uneventful. We slept for some of the journey. People got on and off as the stations came and went. The train halted so many times we lost track of the number. Eventually the scenery changed and we knew we were in Scotland. Craggy mountains, rough gorse and heather dominated our view. It looked bleak and wild.

'I don't like it,' announced Cynthia in a small voice. 'It looks so unfriendly.'

'At least there won't be bombs,' said Lionel. 'I don't like bombs!'

Eventually we chugged into a small station. 'Sneggerton!' shouted the guard. 'Everyone for Sneggerton alight here.' I nudged and prodded the others. 'This is us. We've arrived.'

We jumped down onto the platform with our belongings. No one else got off and there was no one to meet us. Cynthia's eyes began to well up again with tears. 'Do you think they've forgotten us?'

'Of course not,' I reassured her. 'Mother only called Uncle yesterday. Maybe he's busy. We'll ask the guard.'

There was no need. From the distance came the steady clop clopping of a horse's hooves. Leaving the station by means of a small gate we saw a horse lumbering its way up a rutted country lane towards us. The horse was pulling an ancient cart that creaked as it wobbled along. The driver hunched over the reins was unsmiling, just like in the photographs.

It was Uncle Joe. He got down stiffly from the cart and stretched his legs. 'So you've arrived.'

Taking our bags from us, he helped Cynthia into the cart. Lionel and I clambered in after her. 'It's a long way,' he said brusquely. 'You'll find some pies and ale in the basket if you're hungry.' He then climbed back on to the driver's seat, and slapped the reins against the horse's back. The horse ambled off back down the lane. Uncle's rigid back invited no conversation and we sat in silence. Silent tears slid down Cynthia's face while Lionel looked pinched and tense.

The journey was long, but finally an untidy old house loomed before us. Behind the house we could make out farm buildings, a bit of garden and a shimmer of silver.

'That's the loch,' said Uncle Joe. 'It's wide and deep and filled with fish.' Uncle Joe pulled the horse to a halt and knotted the reins to the side of the cart. He helped us and our luggage down then headed for the front door. Before going in he turned abruptly. 'Don't touch anything in the house,' he warned. 'And don't go poking about in any of the rooms.'

It was not the warmest of welcomes. Wearily we followed him in. The hall had a stone floor, a narrow staircase led to the upper floor. Around the hall were other doors. I counted three of them and they were all shut.

Uncle led us up the staircase and then down a long narrow corridor where more doors remained firmly shut. Through a dusty window I could just make out the loch in the distance. Uncle pulled the curtains across the window.

'We might be in Scotland but we obey the blackout,' he warned. He threw open a door. 'You're in here,' he told Cynthia and me, 'and you are to sleep here.' He opened another door further along the passage and showed the room to Lionel. 'The bathroom is just at the end there. Unpack and wash then come down to the kitchen and I'll get you a bite to eat.'

Our room was quite cheerful. Floral curtains covered the wide window and a pretty armchair and table faced it. The beds looked clean and comfortable and the bedspreads matched the curtains. Cynthia did not look so cheerful though.

'I want Mother,' she whispered. 'Will we have to stay here forever, Anne?'

'Only until the war ends. Come on, let's wash, then we'll see if we can find the kitchen.'

I made my way down the corridor to the bathroom. It was, like the bedroom, neat and clean and I wondered how Uncle Joe, living alone, managed to keep it so tidy.

We made our way downstairs and found the kitchen. It was very old-fashioned by our London standards. Pots and pans hung from the rafters and a dresser took up one whole wall. This dresser was covered with cups, plates and bowls. In the middle of the room was a long wooden table. One end had a cloth over it and Uncle had placed an assortment of cold meat, cheese and bread there. There was more food there than we had seen for months.

'Come in,' Uncle Joe beckoned. 'Sit down and help yourselves. I must be off to my work.'

'What do you do?'

'I help out with the war effort.' Uncle was curt. 'Now eat up, it's late.' He left the room.

Before we had finished, Uncle Joe had reappeared, wearing outdoor clothes.

'Go straight up to your rooms when you've eaten. It's a big house and you could get lost,' he warned. 'Keep to your rooms and don't go wandering. Goodbye. I'm off now.'

Questions

Answer the following questions with a full sentence:

1. Where are the children being sent and why?

2. Who do you think is telling the story?

3. What effect does it have on the reader that the story is told in the first person?

4. What do we know about the feelings of the three children as they travel to Scotland?

5. How does the writer convey tension during the farewell at the station?

6. Show evidence from the text that Uncle Joe is not a totally unsympathetic character.

Word work

1. Give the meaning of the following words:

   dominated
   bleak
   loch
   craggy
   brusquely

2. What word was used to describe children who were sent away to live with others during the war?

3. What is the purpose of an '*air raid shelter*'?

Extension work

1. What war was happening when this story took place?

2. We are told that Uncle Joe helps out with the war effort. What do you think his job might be?

3. *"'Don't touch anything in the house,'* he warned. *'And don't go poking about in any of the rooms.'"* Invent a reason why Uncle Joe says this to the children.

4. What is your first impression of Snegworthy? Use the passage to support your view. Say whether you would or would not feel comfortable living there.

5. Imagine you are a government official. You have been asked to give a talk to a group of people about the importance of the blackout. Make notes to help you with your talk, stressing why the blackout is important. Give your talk to your friends.

6. Continue the story. What do the children do next? Think about their relationship with Uncle Joe. Will it change and, if so, how?

Song of the Naga

When the winds soar high over frosted mountains
The song of the Naga rings bright and true.

Mighty are its dragon wings as they beat the cold air,
Brush the tips of trees and make the pine cones fall.

Listen ... do you hear the great throat rumble above the roar of the waterfall?

The smoke from its nostrils mingles with the watery foam.

Tread softly near the nest where lie great eggs, filled with new life.

Listen carefully!

Can you hear the heartbeat?

And the soft murmur of tiny voices as they call their mothers through the shell?

The trees are silent and the whisper of the wind is heard, then lost.

Listen ... do you hear, through the winding pathways of the steep valleys and mountains,

The song of the Naga guiding its kind,

Guiding them home?

66

Questions

Answer the following questions with a full sentence:

1. What is a Naga?

2. What different sounds are referred to in the poem?

3. Judging from the descriptions in the poem, what kind of place does a Naga live in?

4. What do you learn from the poem about the size of a Naga?

5. Who or what is the song of the Naga guiding home?

6. Which phrase do you find most poignant and why?

Word work

List all the words which convey the power of the Naga.

Extension work

1. Why do you think the reader is advised to tread softly near the great eggs?

2. Write a poem of your own about a mythical beast.

3. Write an entry for a book about dragons, describing the Naga and its habitat.

4. Dragons breathe fire and smoke, both of which can be dangerous. Invent a list of safety rules for dragons living together.

Dragon Lore

For those interested in dragons, there is plenty of fascinating literature to explore. One of the most interesting topics is that of the Thayle.

Many people hold that the Thayle dragon is a myth. But for those who have been lucky enough to find one, their existence is as real as the leaves on a tree. Thayles are considered 'kings' of the dragon world. They are not the largest, but are renowned for their intelligence and because they can be trained by humans. In order to train a Thayle, you must find and hatch a Thayle egg, then rear the hatchling successfully. The whole process requires much dedication and, especially after the baby dragon is hatched, great skill and understanding. If the bond between human and dragon is attained, then the rewards are great and you will have a life-long companion and protector. According to the very few people who have been lucky enough to rear and train a Thayle, the creatures become devoted to the person who rears them.

There have been many suggestions as to where the breeding grounds of the Thayles may be found. In his book *Thayle, Truth and Fantasy*, Emerlot Twingbee tells the story of his search for the mysterious Thayle dragon. His journey was a hazardous one, which nearly cost him his life. In this excerpt from the book, Emerlot tells how he finds the breeding ground of the Thayles.

I found myself at the top of a rocky outlet looking down into a vast canyon, through which water gushed at a formidable pace. Daunted, I could see no way of getting down, for

Brilliant Activities for Reading Comprehension, Year 6

the sides were nearly sheer and formed from a crumbly shale which would send any climber crashing down to the jagged rocks below. Then I spotted a gap in the bushes, and noticed that there was animal hair attached to the thorns. Pushing through, I found an animal track, narrow and steep, but well trodden.

Cautiously I made my way down, the thunder of the waterfall ever louder in my ears. Soon I found myself standing beside the waterfall. But how was I to reach the other side? At that moment a deer emerged from the same track I had been following. Startled by sight of me, it ran off. I watched as it bolted through the thick brambles and then disappeared into the very waterfall itself. Dawning comprehension flooded my brain. There must be a path behind the fall of water! Pushing my way

through the cruel thorn after the deer, I scrambled up towards the waterfall. Heavy spray splattered me as I stood beside it. Behind its gushing curtain there was indeed a path, so well concealed it had been invisible to me. I blessed the timely appearance of the deer and pushed through the waterfall.

Finally I emerged on the opposite bank, wet but relieved. Above me, the way to the top appeared tough and daunting. But a small, circling figure in the sky caught my eye. Squinting against the brightness of the sun I saw a tiny, black speck weaving and looping. Transfixed I watched as it seemed to dance in the air. I knew without any doubt that I had found my Thayles.'

Questions

Answer the following questions with a full sentence:

1. What is a Thayle?

2. Do dragons really exist or are they mythical creatures?

3. Is hatching and rearing a baby Thayle easy?

4. What is the name of the book by Emerlot Twingbee?

5. How does the deer help Emerlot?

6. What did Emerlot see that led him to believe he had found his Thayles?

7. Describe some of Emerlot's feelings on his quest.

8. Find another phrase which describes the waterfall.

Word work

1. Give the meaning of the following words:

   myth
   dedication
   canyon
   transfixed
   cautiously
   startled
   daunting

2. *'Transfixed I watched as it seemed to dance in the air.'* In your own words describe what is meant by this sentence.

3. If something is *'well trodden'*, what does this tell you?

Extension work

1. *'Dawning comprehension flooded my brain. There must be a path behind the fall of water!'* Rewrite these sentences in your own words.

2. Choose three adjectives from the passage that you think enhance the story. What does each one mean?

3. If Emerlot Twingbee finds a Thayle egg, what challenges do you think he will encounter when incubating, hatching and rearing the dragon?

4. Imagine you are Emerlot Twingbee. Describe any part of your journey to find the Thayles.

5. There are many types of dragon. Make up names for them and briefly describe their different characteristics.

Brilliant Activities for Reading Comprehension, Year 6
© Charlotte Makhlouf and Brilliant Publications Limited

Stately Phantoms

CHAPTER ONE

There was a time when I did not believe in ghosts. It makes me laugh to think of it now. I was so naïve. Then I met Penelope.

It was at a musical evening at Rednock Manor. The owners, Lynda and Taz Hope, had recently opened up the house to the public. A string quartet in the minstrels' gallery played music by Beethoven, Schubert and Brahms while we sat below in the comfortable hall.

During the interval I talked with the other guests. One of these was Penelope, a tall woman in an elegant black gown, with flaming auburn hair. I introduced myself to her and learnt, amongst other things, that she was an artist. In fact, the owners of the house had quite a few of her pictures. She pointed to a small painting which hung beside the stone fireplace. It showed a farmyard cat licking itself on a stone wall, which was bathed in golden sunshine. The artist clearly had a feel for light and shadow and the whole composition had a warmth and intensity about it.

'The cat was called Linus,' Penelope told me. 'He was a fabulous hunter. He's dead now, but he used to do a wonderful job keeping down the rat population on the farm.' I wanted to ask Penelope more about her work, but the interval was over, and we had to take our places. I tried to find her again at the end of the evening, but when I looked around for her, she was nowhere to be seen.

The Hopes appeared confused when I asked them about Penelope. 'She painted that picture over there by the fireplace,' I told them. 'She was the tall woman in the black dress. I talked to her in the interval.'

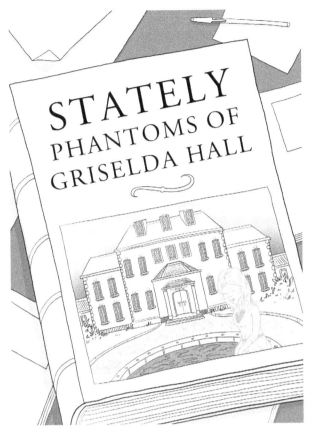

'Oh, Penelope,' Mr Hope smiled. 'You must mean Penelope Fitzwilliam. But she's been dead for over fifty years.'

* * * * *

It took me a while to come to terms with the idea that I had been speaking to a ghost. At first the idea seemed impossible. But after further investigations, I realised that not only was there no guest that evening called Penelope, but no one else had seen a tall woman in black.

'Her name was Penelope Fitzwilliam,' Mr Hope told me. 'She lived here in the early twentieth century until her tragic death. She tried to rescue her cat from the river, but the weeds pulled her under and she drowned. My wife and I have never seen her, but other people have mentioned seeing an auburn-haired woman in the grounds. She was a very talented artist who had a great love of animals, especially cats.'

When I thought about my encounter with Penelope, I suddenly found I could remember little details. Penelope had not been drinking any wine or juice, unlike all the other guests. There had been something shadowy about her, I could see that now, something that made her look 'other-worldly'.

To try to make sense of my experience, I went to see Henrietta Williams, an authority on the supernatural. When I explained what had happened she asked for more details. What had Penelope been wearing? What was the atmosphere around her like? How had the other guests responded to me whilst I was talking with her? I found these last two questions of particular interest. While talking with Penelope I had not paid much attention to the atmosphere, but when prompted by Henrietta, I realised that the temperature around us had been significantly cooler than anywhere else, as if a draught were swirling about us. And when I had left Penelope to return to my seat, I noticed that one or two faces around me looked slightly puzzled. It had not bothered me at the time, but now I realised they must have thought I was talking to myself!

After talking to Henrietta, I decided to find out more about the spirits to be found in many of our stately homes. The people who have been most helpful are the guides who spend their time showing visitors round these ancient houses.

I began with Joan Witherspoon, who has been a guide at Toorock Castle for the past twelve years. Toorock Castle is an impressive dwelling on the Devon coast. It stands on a rugged cliff, surrounded by wild moorland, and used to be the haunt of smugglers.

Joan was only too happy to tell me of her strange experiences.

'We get a surprising number of visitors,' Joan told me, 'considering it is so bleak here. Some visitors arrive by boat; they sail around the headland and the boat moors in the bay. The sightseers get rowed over to the little beach, then there's a steep climb up the steps in the cliff. It's a romantic way to begin the guided tour because they get the feel of what it must have been like for the old smugglers.'

She went on, 'We know that Toorock has plenty of ghosts, not only because people have seen them but because of strange occurrences.' She then told me about what had happened to a woman called Iris Delafield.

'Iris was American. She was rather bothered by the hot weather we were having. I was showing her group around the herb garden when she must have lost her way and gone through the side gate. Iris sat down on a boulder at the edge of the cliff and looked out to sea. She saw a couple of rowing boats coming to land and six strangely dressed men get out of them. They were carrying barrels, which they took up the beach and left in a cave in the cliffside. She watched for some time until the boats had disappeared again, round the headland. Then she came back to the herb garden, where I and the rest of her party waited for her. She had been gone for no more than a few minutes, and yet Iris swears she had been sitting on that boulder for over half an hour watching the men. When the visitors went back down to the beach on their way home, I took the opportunity and went with them. I checked the cave and found no barrels there at all. It was completely empty.'

Questions

Answer the following questions with a full sentence:

1. Where did the writer meet Penelope?

2. What was striking about Penelope? Why did the writer notice her?

3. Describe what the writer learnt about Penelope on the evening of the concert.

4. What did the writer learn about Penelope later on?

5. Why did some of the other people at the concert look puzzled?

6. Who was Iris and where was she visiting?

7. What did Iris see that was strange?

8. Who is Henrietta Williams? What three specific details did she ask for?

Word work

1. Give the meaning of the following words:

   naïve
   auburn
   tragic
   smuggler
   encounter
   headland

2. What is a *'minstrels' gallery'*?

3. What is a *'phantom'*?

Extension work

1. Which words or phrases tell us that Iris' encounter is peculiar?

2. In your own words, explain why Toorock is a popular tourist attraction.

3. Is Griselda's book the type of genre which would appeal to you? Give reasons for your answer.

4. Imagine you are Griselda. Write another chapter for her book.

5. Imagine you are someone who Griselda wants to interview about your ghostly experience at a stately home. Write about your experience in detail, saying what happened and how you felt.

6. Write a story about smugglers at Toorock.

7. Why is arriving by boat at Toorock considered to be a romantic experience?

The Case of the Missing Turtle

(A Miss Wimpole case)

The Chudleigh village fête had been in full swing since ten that morning. We were blessed with fine weather and from my excellent position beside the tea tent I had a marvellous view of proceedings.

Reverend Sally was the main organiser of the fête. She held it yearly in aid of the Widows and Orphans Benevolent Fund. Of course, Reverend Sally did not run the fête alone. She had a team of willing and determined ladies who shouldered much of the responsibility. It was this team, headed by the indomitable Miss Hartley, who chivvied the village into a frenzy of making and baking and donating in order that the fête be a success.

I myself had knitted a number of small items for Mr Lamb's stall, while Mrs Edgar had made most of the cakes and buns on her stall. I could see her smiling and laughing with a couple of ladies as they chose their purchases and Mrs Edgar popped them into bags.

The stalls were not just devoted to selling things. Mrs Rose was doing a grand job with the coconut shy and Mr and Mrs Wilkins were helping young Emily Finch to hook a duck. There was a book stall and a flower stall and for the first time Mr Graves was running a bric-a-brac stall. All manner of quaint and curious items had been donated and several were very interesting. One item in particular stood out, a small, silver turtle, donated by Doctor Hesketh. Unable to attend the event due to ill health, she had donated the turtle; she said it had once belonged to her mother. The turtle was decorated with coloured stones and its back opened to reveal a secret compartment in which earrings could be kept. As Mrs Bunting sold me a cup of tea she told me she had just bought the turtle as a present for her sister, but had requested that Mr Graves look after it until she was free to collect it.

Among all this jollity and good humour only Miss Hartley stood aloof. Her pinched face surveyed the proceedings with sour disapproval. Every now and then she would appear to hover around a stall, enquiring into how much had been sold.

I sipped my tea and nibbled my cake, glad of the opportunity to rest my weary legs and bask in the sun.

'Ah, Miss Wimpole!' said a voice behind me. I turned in surprise.

'Mr Simpkins!' I exclaimed. 'Back from your travels, I see. How are you?'

Mr Simpkins beamed, his tanned face exuding health and vigour. 'Very well … very well indeed, thank you.'

I gestured to the vacant chair beside me, and Mr Simpkins sank into it gratefully.

Brilliant Activities for Reading Comprehension, Year 6
© Charlotte Makhlouf and Brilliant Publications Limited

'And how was Egypt?' I asked. 'Did you have a pleasant trip?'

Mr Simpkins' face lit up with enthusiasm. 'It was excellent, most interesting. A trip I shall remember for the rest of my life. I bought a model pyramid that opens up. And I took so many photographs during my visit to the Valley of the Kings, the children at school will be looking at them for weeks!'

I smiled at him indulgently. Mr Simpkins taught in Chudleigh Primary School and when travelling he always brought back exciting things to show them.

'I had a ride in one of those sailing boats they call feluccas,' he continued. 'The Nile was most beautiful. But I saw no crocodiles.'

'Will you show me your pictures?' I touched him on the arm. 'It would remind me of my youth and the time I spent there as a young girl.'

Mr Simpkins beamed. 'Of course, Miss Wimpole, nothing would give me greater pleasure.' At that moment he looked up and frowned slightly. I turned quickly and followed his gaze to the bric-a-brac stall where a small crowd had gathered.

'I wonder what is going on there?'

Suddenly there was a scream and a woman's voice shouted:

'He's dead … Sydney's dead!'

Mr Simpkins stared at me in horror. We got up hastily and made our way to the stall. A little crowd of people had gathered about it. I could see Miss Hartley's hatchet face staring disgustedly at a figure lying crumpled over the table. Reverend Sally was also there, her face filled with dismay.

Slumped over his bric-a-brac was Mr Graves, his eyes wide and staring. On one side of his head a thin trickle of blood seeped from a nasty gash.

While others called the police and ambulance, I looked through the scattered pieces of glass and pottery from his stall. I knew he had been asked to keep the turtle safe for Mrs Bunting. But there was no sign of the little silver animal. It had completely vanished.

Questions

Answer the following questions with a full sentence:

1. Why is the village fête held?

2. Who are the real organisers of the fête?

3. How do we know that Miss Wimpole is not a young woman?

4. How has Miss Wimpole contributed to the village fête?

5. Who is Sydney and how has he died?

6. Describe the features which make the turtle special.

7. What do you learn about the relationship between Miss Wimpole and Mr Simpkins from their conversation together?

8. Why do you think that Miss Wimpole 'looked through the scattered pieces of glass and pottery' from the stall?

9. Why do you think Miss Hartley is 'staring disgustedly' at Sydney?

10. Describe three things Mr Simpkins did when he was in Egypt.

Extension work

1. Why do you think Miss Wimpole considers the tea tent to be 'an excellent position'?

2. If you were asked to set up a stall at a fête or fair, what kind of stall would you choose and why?

3. Why or how do you think the turtle has vanished?

4. We know that Mr Simpkins is a schoolteacher. What do you think Miss Wimpole does? Justify your response.

5. What do you think will happen next in the story? Continue it yourself.

6. Have you got a special possession? Describe what it is and why it is special to you.

7. Reverend Sally is an imposter! Describe who she really is and what she is really doing in Chudleigh.

8. Compare and contrast the language used in this passage with that of Stately Phantoms. How is it similar/different?

Word work

Give the meaning of the following words:

frenzy
bric-a-brac
quaint
reveal
gash

The Cookery Competition

There were eight finalists in the 'Cook off'. Denzel was one of the eight. Looking at the confident, poised people around him, Denzel wondered how he had managed to reach the final. Everyone else was much older than him. They all seemed to wear the same smug, self-satisfied expressions and they barely spoke to one another. He wondered whether they felt it was beneath their dignity to speak to anyone else. Were their recipes so brilliant they had to be kept 'Top Secret'?

As Denzel stood by his workstation he focused his mind on the recipes which had taken him to this final. The judges had praised his melt-in-the-mouth steak and kidney pudding and eulogised over his fruit sorbet topped with spun sugar. But that spun sugar had nearly been a disaster. He had only prevented the sugar from burning by whipping it off the heat and plunging it into a pan of cold water.

Denzel shook his head and swept yesterday's recipes from his mind. He must focus on his next creations, that he had practised for weeks in the kitchen at home. They would make three dishes today: a starter, a main course and a dessert. Denzel had opted for simplicity rather than complexity. As his final course he was going to make a plain, traditional rice pudding. His strategy was risky, because everyone else was sure to create something delicate and complicated, but a perfect rice pudding would complement his other dishes beautifully.

Denzel was less sure about his main course: Beef Wellington. It would be so easy to overcook the pastry on the outside and leave the meat on the inside underdone. Denzel had made eight Beef Wellingtons before he was satisfied with his technique. But would the judges like it? With the beef, he planned to put some asparagus and a neat mound of creamed potato. He had grown the potatoes in his own garden, a variety that tasted delicious; he had dug them up only that morning.

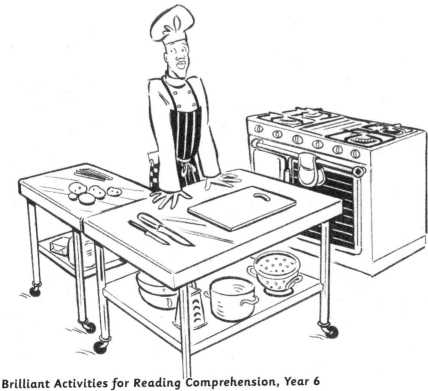

Denzel's starter was the most complicated of all his dishes. He had thought long and hard before deciding on a salmon paté garnished with chives. He had caught the salmon himself, only the day before. Denzel felt awkward about the salmon. His face reddened at the mere thought of it. It had come from the river at the bottom of his garden, only the fishing rights to the river did not belong to him but to his neighbour, Henry Tomkinson. Henry Tomkinson was known to have an unpleasant temper, and he feverishly guarded the fish in his river against poachers. Fishing in Tomkinson's stretch of the river was only allowed after you had paid a considerable sum of money – and even then you might sit for hours waiting for the fish to bite, and go home empty-handed. Denzel had not paid – he had crept down to the bottom of the garden and, under cover of the dense bushes, had waded into the water with a net. To his surprise, the river was teeming with fish. Denzel had quickly scooped up a salmon and retreated to the safety of his house.

Denzel shivered at the thought of his theft and busied himself with his workstation, reminding himself how the various machines worked. He glanced furtively at the seven other workstations. They were ranged around the enormous hall. Despite the heat from the mass of lights above, Denzel shivered again. They had only four hours in which to make all their dishes. As soon as the bell sounded they must stop cooking, even if they had not completed their menu. Denzel found his tummy churning with nerves. He wished the judges would arrive so they could start cooking and he could forget his nerves. He thought about how much he wanted to win the competition. Not just to prove that he was a good cook but because of the prize: an all expenses paid trip to Cape Town, with visits to famous vineyards, and the chance to work in the kitchen of the famous chef, Jonas Denglan. The trip also included three nights at a game reserve in the Kruger National Park. Denzel had never been to a game reserve. It was one of his dreams.

The doors to the hall opened and the five judges appeared. Denzel stopped daydreaming and focused on the people entering the hall. He recognised none of them. They lined up on the platform at the back of the room and looked unsmilingly at the contestants. The presenter began introducing them all. Two of the judges were celebrity cooks. They were casually dressed and smiled briefly as they were introduced. There was also a critic from a newspaper and some woman from an organic food shop. Denzel switched off briefly until the final judge was announced.

'Henry Tomkinson is a well-known connoisseur of fine food and wine. He is our final judge today.'

Denzel felt the blood drain from his face. Henry Tomkinson! Of all the bad luck.

Denzel's eyes went to the fridge. Lying there, oblivious to the tension outside, was one of Henry's salmon.

Brilliant Activities for Reading Comprehension, Year 6
© Charlotte Makhlouf and Brilliant Publications Limited

Questions

Answer the following questions with a full sentence:

1. What dishes will Denzel be creating for the competition?

2. Why do you think Denzel is feeling under pressure?

3. At what point does *'the blood drain'* from Denzel's face and why?

4. Briefly describe what we know about Henry Tomkinson's character.

5. Briefly describe what we know about Denzel's character.

6. How do we know that Denzel has worked hard to prepare for this final?

7. What possible problems does Denzel face with his Beef Wellington?

8. What do we learn about Denzel's feelings towards the other competitors?

Extension work

1. How does the writer convey tension in the passage?

2. Out of all the dishes Denzel plans to make, which do you think will prove the most difficult and why?

3. Do you feel Denzel was justified in obtaining his salmon the way he did? Give reasons for your response.

4. If you were one of the judges, what would you be looking for in the competitors' dishes?

5. Half way through the competition, the judges move around the room, chatting to the competitors as they cook. Henry Tomkinson visits Denzel's workstation and asks him why he chose to make a salmon paté and where he got his fish. What do you think Denzel will say to Henry Tomkinson?

6. Imagine you are Denzel. Write an account of how you got the fish from the river.

7. What do you think will happen to Denzel? Write what you think will happen next in the competition.

Word work

Give the meaning of the following words:

poised
self-satisfied
eulogised
connoisseur
traditional

Shopping Centre Opens

The Daily Platform

DESPITE HUGE opposition from locals, the new Happyfields shopping centre at Bromley-on-Tyne has now opened. Mayor, Ms Davina Porter, who officially opened the centre, has supported the scheme from the outset, saying it will provide more choice to the people of Bromley-on-Tyne. Yesterday, as Ms Porter cut the crimson ribbon across its main escalators, and declared the centre open, 8000 red and yellow balloons were released into the sky.

This vast steel and glass complex boasts 49 shops, three supermarkets, car parking for 1000 cars, and a cinema with six screens. The old Portly Street cinema only has two screens and with the arrival of the new complex, its future is uncertain. Matthew Deakin, who runs the old cinema, said yesterday, 'Of course people want more choice, but we always have a regular turnover of new films; and our classic nights, when we show the old black and whites, are very popular. But with this new cinema I'm not sure we'll manage to stay open.' However, the feasibility of the new cinema is itself uncertain – the auditoria are small and the price of a cinema ticket is much higher than at Portly Street.

Brilliant Activities for Reading Comprehension, Year 6
© Charlotte Makhlouf and Brilliant Publications Limited

Yesterday, Happyfields was filled with people eager to see what it had to offer. The complex boasts a large number of lifts and escalators. On its opening day, however, the lifts were not working due to a technical fault, which made life troublesome for those with prams and buggies.

Happyfields' huge steel and glass domed roof contrasts greatly with the simple cottages and houses around. Dunwitch and Nutty, the building contractors, are delighted with the completion of a project which has taken seven years. 'There were numerous problems to work through,' explained Ludwig Dunwitch, 'but once we had amended our plans, it all worked perfectly. The project has been very satisfying and has given work to a large number of local people.'

Mr Dunwitch refused to elaborate on the 'numerous problems' but everyone in Bromley-on-Tyne is aware of these. One problem was the opposition by local people who felt they had enough shops already in what is, after all, a fairly small town, and who resented the idea that their streets and homes would be dwarfed by what has been dubbed 'the glass eyesore'.

Another problem involved the siting of the complex. The planners wanted to build the centre on the old Bromley-on-Tyne football ground, which is used by local schools for a range of activities. Fortunately for the children, the shopping complex was eventually positioned behind the old furniture workshops, where an area of wasteland had been lying idle for some time.

Bromley-on-Tyne is a small town in a rural area and not particularly well-off. Doubters wonder whether the new shopping centre will survive, when so many of its new shops cater for the more affluent individual. Whether the council has made the right decision in allowing this new building, only time will tell.

Questions

Answer the following questions with a full sentence:

1. Explain what a shopping complex is.

2. What reason has been given to justify building 'Happyfields'?

3. What initial problems did the project face?

4. Why do you think Ludwig Dunwitch was reluctant to discuss these problems?

5. What difficulties is the shopping centre likely to face in the future?

6. List the ways in which 'Happyfields' will be a positive contribution to the community.

7. List the ways in which 'Happyfields' will not be a positive contribution to the community.

Word work

Give the meaning of the following words:

opposition
vast
numerous
siting
dwarfed
dubbed
affluent

Extension work

1. Choice plays an important part in the development and future of Happyfields. In your own words, describe what choices are being offered.

2. Why is the future of the Portly Street cinema uncertain?

3. In your opinion what is the most challenging problem Happyfields is likely to face and why?

4. If you could give Happyfields an alternative name, what would you choose and why?

The Dark Side

Lucy heard the voices long, long before she ever saw them.

She was lying huddled under a large cardboard box when a soft voice whispered to her. The sweetness of the voice jolted her into wakefulness and so real was its presence she looked around for the owner. There was no one. Not far away Old Ned snored blissfully, unaware of anything, surrounded by a pile of stinking clothes that he swore helped to block out the wind.

Lucy had joined the beggars when she was only eight. Her 'home' had varied over the past two years, as the group sought to evade capture by the secret street police. This secret force had started rounding up people who lived on the streets and the jails were filling rapidly with unkempt creatures who longed for their old freedom. So far Lucy had managed to evade capture, and a beating, by being quick-witted and nimble.

Lucy had taken to the streets by necessity. Her mother had died when she was a baby and she had never known her father. The orphanage where she was placed was a soulless place, where the older children looked after the younger and where food was scarce and beatings plentiful. In desperation, Lucy had escaped in a laundry van with a boy called Charlie. Neither of them had wanted to be sold to the abattoir man, Macgregor Smythe.

Macgregor Smythe had arrived at the orphanage one day, unannounced. He was a huge, florid man with dark, bristly hair and a cruel, shifty face. He said he was on the lookout for a couple of children to help in his butchering shed on the outskirts of the city. All the children had been lined up and Macgregor Smythe had eyed them all. His eyes had lingered over Lucy and Charlie and the blood had drained from Lucy's face when she saw the vile man nod and jerk his head at her. Lucy cringed at the thought of being sent to work there, for she loved animals.

That night she and Charlie escaped in the laundry truck, half suffocated by the piles of dirty sheets they heaped over themselves. Long before they reached the laundry they jumped out and furtively walked the streets until they found shelter under a railway bridge. In the morning Charlie had left her.

'I'm going to find my Auntie Maureen,' he had told Lucy. 'I know she lives up north somewhere in a village called Tidworth. It'll be safer there than it is here.'

Charlie warned Lucy about the police before he left. 'They're special police,' he warned, 'not like the others because they don't have a uniform so you don't know who they are. They're on the lookout for beggars; I heard them talking about it at the orphanage. They say they're cleaning up the streets and all beggars are to go to jail. Good luck to you, Lucy.'

That had been two years ago and Lucy did not know whether Charlie had found his Auntie Maureen. In those two years she had had problems of her own. The beggars had their own underworld which had been difficult to infiltrate. Places she thought she could sleep in turned out to be 'homes' for other beggars and were jealously guarded and fought over. In those two years she learnt how to fight and hunt and she paid her money to the underworld king so that her place in the beggars' kingdom was assured.

Dustbins provided her suppers. Sometimes a kindly café owner took pity on her and gave her leftover food or scraps. The bins outside restaurants were a favourite place for finding food but they were dangerous too. Lucy had narrowly escaped with her life in an alley behind a large restaurant. Three adult beggars were there already and they were not willing to share their pickings with a child. One of the beggars had challenged Lucy with a knife and she ran for her life. The scar she bore on her neck reminded her of this incident and the need to be cunning.

It had been Old Ned who had taken the girl under his wing.

That was the day when the police nearly caught up with her. She had been in the marketplace, her stomach growling with hunger. The sight of so much food and drink was hard to bear, especially the table laden with pies fresh from the oven. Their aroma wafted tantalisingly into the air and Lucy could not prevent her thin fingers stretching out to take one. She thought the crowd would mask her from view but a large woman had spotted her and started to cry 'stop thief'. Lucy ran, ran as fast as her spindly legs would carry her, her heart hammering in her chest and her lungs gasping for breath.

She realised she was being chased by men with mean, hard faces who moved with surprising speed and seemed to know where she was going. She dodged through the crowds then took to a maze of narrow lanes, but at the end of a dark alleyway she came to a dead end. Terrified, she looked left and right but

Brilliant Activities for Reading Comprehension, Year 6
© Charlotte Makhlouf and Brilliant Publications Limited

there was no means of escape and at the entrance to the alleyway the street police waited.

Then, from out of the gloom, a hand reached down from over the top of the wall and a voice hissed, 'Up here, girl!' Lucy took the proffered hand and found herself being hauled over the wall by a man with great strength. It was Old Ned. At the time, there were no introductions or explanations. The old man took Lucy deep into the sewers where they hid until the streets were clear. For the first time in ages, Lucy felt safe. Old Ned became her protector. He showed the girl the secret places where the police would never find them and it was then that Lucy began hearing the voices.

The cardboard box had been Lucy's bed for a couple of months. As she wriggled out of it, she looked around. Old Ned was the only person in view. There was no one else beneath the motorway bridge. Lucy rubbed her head. She was imagining things. The rain must have chilled her more than she realised, that and the lack of food. Her stomach churned with hunger, for supper last night was a single piece of stale bread.

'Come with us,' whispered a voice, 'and you'll have all the food you can eat.'

Lucy whipped around. The voice was right beside her and yet there was no one there. The voice continued, soft and sweet and deeply persuasive. 'You will be warm too, warm forever, and you will want for nothing.'

'Who are you?' snapped Lucy, fear gripping her. 'Show yourselves!'

A hand fell onto her shoulder and she jumped.

'Ned!' She almost collapsed with relief.

'Is anything the matter, girl? I heard you speak.'

Lucy frowned, her eyes darting backwards and forwards. 'I don't think so,' she muttered. 'I thought I heard a voice. It was calling to me.' Old Ned froze. His face hardened and his eyes filled with alarm. The hand on Lucy's shoulder tightened in warning.

'Don't listen to them, girl. Do you hear me? Block them out. They'll do you no good. They're from the Dark Side.'

Questions

Answer the following questions with a full sentence:

1. Why did Lucy live in an orphanage?

2. Who is Macgregor Smythe and what did he want from Lucy?

3. How does Lucy leave the orphanage?

4. How do we know that life on the streets is hard for Lucy?

5. Why is eating food from dustbins dangerous?

6. Who were the *'men with mean, hard faces'* who chased Lucy?

7. In your own words, describe how Lucy met Old Ned.

8. What do you think Old Ned means by the 'Dark Side' and why is he quick to caution against it?

9. How old is Lucy when Ned tells her about the Dark Side?

Extension work

1. How does the writer maintain the element of suspense in the passage?

2. Which part of the passage intrigues you the most and why?

3. List the things Lucy has learnt in order to survive on the streets.

4. Do you think Lucy made the right decision to leave the orphanage? Give reasons for your answer.

5. Find two sentences in the passage, which you feel best describe the hopelessness of Lucy's situation.

6. If you could give the passage another title, what would it be and why?

7. Imagine you are Lucy. Continue the story from your point of view.

8. We are told that Lucy has to pay money to the underworld king. What do you think this is and why does she have to pay?

Word work

Give the meaning of the following words:

abattoir
orphanage
unkempt
infiltrate
tantalisingly
protector

Everest

A dangerous place

Everest, in the high Himalayas, stands tall and firm, a giant unmoved by wind or snow, the air too thin for plant or animal life. Climbing Mount Everest is hard and dangerous work. Even with the aid of modern technology, the fittest of climbers may experience the effects of hypoxia. Then their dreams of reaching the summit of the highest mountain in the world are over.

Cerebral hypoxia is caused by lack of oxygen to the brain. People with cerebral hypoxia show signs of impaired judgement; they become confused and as their condition worsens they do not know where they are or what they are doing. People who recover from this type of hypoxia remember going into a trance-like state in which events and objects were magnified out of proportion. But many do not recover. In 1996 eight people died in a single day on Everest.

Research is underway to find out more about the effects of altitude on the human body. Scientists are interested to understand why people's abilities in mountain conditions vary so much. Some climbers on Everest can trudge through heavy snow and climb cliffs at their maximum capacity for hours without even the assistance of oxygen. Others struggle to breathe in the thin air; some collapse and are unable to carry on. These scientists know that the larger the lungs, the more oxygen the lungs can absorb. This oxygen is in turn picked up by the blood and delivered to the muscle tissues. Perhaps this is an important clue to people's varying abilities.

Adjusting your body to the thin air, allowing it to get used to lower levels of oxygen, is vital if a climber wants to tackle Mount Everest. On early expeditions to Mount Everest, climbers trekked for weeks to get to Base Camp, which gave people's bodies time to adjust. Today, climbers are flown into Lukla, a Sherpa village from where it takes just ten days to reach Base Camp. This shortens the amount of time a climber has to acclimatise to the thin air.

The climb

Once at Everest Base Camp, there follows a period of further acclimatisation. Base Camp is situated on a glacier that constantly shifts and moves beneath your feet. It is an inhospitable place filled with the brightly coloured tents of climbers who are anxious to make it to the top.

The climb to Mount Everest's summit begins with a traverse of the Khumbu Icefall. This is a steep glacier filled with deep crevasses and huge ice blocks. It should be climbed in the early morning when the sun has not yet warmed the snow and ice. A mass of fixed ropes and ladders cross the crevasses to enable climbers to get across the glacier; without them, no climber would make it through. It is a dangerous start to the climb, for the icefall is unpredictable. The giant blocks of ice which dominate the area can weigh up to thirty tons each. These blocks can shift without warning; and crevasses can cave in, taking climbers with them. Later in the day the icefall becomes even more unpredictable and unstable; to cross it then would be foolhardy in the extreme.

Climbing higher, one faces further risks, such as acute mountain sickness. The early signs of this are a headache followed by dizziness, trouble sleeping and nausea. A person may lose their appetite and be reluctant to drink. As the sickness develops, the nausea continues, and sufferers begin to have problems with their balance and coordination. Should these symptoms appear, it is important that the climber seeks immediate medical advice and goes back down the mountain for a while to a place where lower altitude will allow the body a chance to recover and adjust.

Climbers say that in acute mountain sickness, the shortage of breath and lack of sleep are the two most troublesome things. The sickness can attack very quickly. One minute you feel strong and well and the next you are stricken with a severe headache.

It takes time for the body to adapt, but eventually climbers make it up to the high camps and then prepare for their attempt on the summit. At 26,000 feet they face the Death Zone; this is aptly named because here the body uses up its store of oxygen faster than it can be replenished. Sleeping becomes a problem. The muscles begin to waste away and a climber's weight decreases. The body becomes weaker and weaker, so much so that their time above 26,000 feet is severely limited. An extended stay in the Death Zone without extra oxygen will end in death.

Those climbers who reach the summit of Mount Everest achieve a great dream, but not without a price. They will have pushed their bodies to the utmost and suffered discomforts most of us can not imagine. They have, however, reached the Top of the World and that is an experience most of us will only ever read about.

Brilliant Activities for Reading Comprehension, Year 6
© Charlotte Makhlouf and Brilliant Publications Limited

Questions

Answer the following questions with a full sentence:

1. In which mountain range is Mount Everest?

2. What causes hypoxia?

3. What symptoms does a person with cerebral hypoxia show?

4. Why might climbers with large lungs be at an advantage?

5. Why is the Khumbu Icefall so hazardous?

6. What helps climbers to cross the crevasses in the icefall?

7. Where is the Death Zone located?

8. Why is the Death Zone given that name?

Word work

1. Give the meaning of the following words:

   crevasse
   traverse
   glacier
   maximum
   decrease

2. If your judgement is *'impaired'*, what does that mean?

3. If a place is considered *'inhospitable'*, what does that mean?

4. What does it mean to be *'acclimatised'*?

Extension work

1. From what you have read, do you think climbing Mount Everest sounds appealing? Give reasons for your answer.

2. From what you have read, do you think it would have been better to have joined one of the old expeditions or a modern one? Give reasons for your response.

3. Given that there are significant dangers to climbing at high altitude, what do you think attracts people to high mountains?

4. Why would a shortage of breath and a lack of sleep be a problem on Mount Everest?

5. We are told that climbers who reach the summit achieve a *'great dream, but not without a price,'* explain what you think is meant by this expression and what *'the price'* could be?

6. Which two phrases best describe how dangerous Everest is?

7. How do you think the research that has been gathered will benefit climbers in the future?

The Formula (part 1)

The scene is an animal laboratory. There are rows of cages containing guinea pigs, rats, rabbits and mice. At one side of the room is a long table with test tubes, beakers and other equipment. At the table, wearing white coats, are two people. They are Professor Patek and her laboratory technician, Cornelius Helm. On the table in front of them is a large brown and white guinea pig.

Professor (*in a low voice*) This is incredible! Are you quite sure, Cornelius?

Cornelius (*frightened*) Of course I'm sure! Why don't you poke it again and see.

Guinea pig I'd rather you didn't. It hurts.

Cornelius (*going pale*) There you are… . It spoke again.

Professor (*looking furtively around*) Quick. Shut the door and lock it. We don't want anyone coming in. This is amazing. A speaking guinea pig!

(Cornelius scuttles to the door and locks it.)

Professor Now, Cornelius, tell me exactly how much of Dipopsonocum N2134D you gave to this animal. Be exact. It's clear that our success is due to giving the correct dosage.

Cornelius (*shakily*) These guinea pigs had the lowest dosage, every day for the last four weeks, except at night time. At night they had a meal of guinea pig mix from the pet shop. I've logged it all in the record book.

Guinea pig (*in a bored voice*) That's not quite true now, Cornelius, is it?

Professor (*startled*) I beg your pardon.

Guinea pig He's not telling the truth. It wasn't the lowest dosage. He gave us a whole pipette full. He got bored measuring out such tiny amounts so he just simplified the dose. That meant he had time to pop off to watch the football on the TV in the canteen.

Professor Cornelius, what is going on here? Not only am I having to cope with a talking guinea pig (*she lowers her voice conspiratorially*) but the animal is informing me that the dosage was completely wrong.

Cornelius (*apologetically*) If I might explain, Professor.

Professor Please do, Cornelius, please do. I will be speaking to the Board of Oral Research in a few days

Brilliant Activities for Reading Comprehension, Year 6

© Charlotte Makhlouf and Brilliant Publications Limited

Cornelius time and I need to be absolutely sure of my facts before I do.

Cornelius I gave them one eighth of a pipette full of the drug. Honestly.

Guinea pig Tut, tut, tut. Naughty Cornelius! You know you couldn't be bothered with all that measuring. We heard you say so only last week. Bernard and Marcia were not impressed. But the effect hasn't been too bad. Simon can read Dr Hiroswami's book about *The Future of the Universe* which you've often left lying on the table. He didn't care for it, by the way. You should talk to him yourself, Professor. Simon has some interesting opinions on the universe and its future.

Professor (*staring at the guinea pig*) But this is absolutely astounding. An intelligent guinea pig, which is able to converse with a human. You gave the other guinea pigs names … What do you call yourself?

Guinea pig Delilah.

Professor There is much I would like to ask you, Delilah, about the treatment you have all been receiving. I would be interested to hear how it has made you feel and what changes you have experienced within your bodies.

Delilah And we have questions to ask you, Professor. My first is: when do you intend to release us?

Professor Release you … what do you mean 'release you'? Well I …

Delilah So you don't intend to release

us. I see. That leads to my second question. If you don't intend to release us, what do you intend to do with us?

Professor (*excitedly*) You are of great importance to the scientific world. I, Professor Ramona Patek, have invented a formula that can make small animals speak, and enhances their intelligence. The world will be astounded. Perhaps I can move on to working with larger creatures … dogs or horses.

Delilah (*sceptically*) They may be astounded. But will they be pleased? Do you think that the world will want animals to possess exceptional intelligence? What might the results be for humans?

Professor (*her expression hardening*) I can see that animals would be deeply annoying if they all turned out like you! Cornelius, lock the creature away in its cage with the others and come with me. I want you to outline all that you have done with the animals in the last twenty-four hours.

(*Cornelius puts Delilah in her cage. The Professor and Cornelius exit.*)

Delilah (*to the other guinea pigs*) Did you hear it all? Marcia? Bernard? Simon?

Marcia (*nodding*) They'll have to kill us, eventually. I could see the Professor's face when you asked her where humans would be if animals possessed great intelligence. We must leave this lab, before it is too late!

Questions

Answer the following questions with a full sentence:

1. Where does the action take place?

2. How has it come about that Delilah, the guinea pig, can speak?

3. What particularly intelligent thing has Simon been doing?

4. What do we learn from Delilah about the dosage the guinea pigs have been given, and how is this significant?

5. Why does the Professor need to be *'absolutely sure'* of her facts?

6. Does Delilah think *'the world'* will be pleased that animals can be given exceptional intelligence?

Word work

Give the meaning of the following words:

furtively
dosage
simplified
converse

Extension work

1. What are stage directions and how do they help a play's actors or readers?

2. *'It wasn't the lowest dosage. He gave us a whole pipette full. He got bored measuring out such tiny amounts so he just simplified the dose.'* Why do you think that the dosage is so important to the Professor?

3. Delilah says that humans *'may be astounded'* about the result of the Professor's experiment. She goes on, *'But will they be pleased? Do you think that the world will want animals to possess exceptional intelligence? What might the results be for humans?'* What do you think the result might be for humans if animals could speak?

4. How many guinea pigs are introduced to us altogether?

5. What do you notice about the way in which Delilah speaks to Cornelius?

6. For what reasons might the Professor lower her voice *'conspiratorially'*?

7. What do we learn about Cornelius' personality from the passage?

8. If you could rename the passage, what would you call it and why?

Brilliant Activities for Reading Comprehension, Year 6
© *Charlotte Makhlouf and Brilliant Publications Limited*

The Formula (part 2)

The scene is inside the laboratory. It is night time. Professor Patek is seated at the long table looking through a microscope. Beside her, yawning deeply, is her laboratory technician, Cornelius Helm. Inside their cage, watching the humans carefully are the guinea pigs: Delilah, Marcia, Bernard and Simon.

Professor (*She pushes back the microscope and glares at Cornelius.*) I think I'll turn in for the night now, Cornelius. See to it that all the cages are locked and that my notepad is put in the filing cabinet along with the other documents. Lock it! It's my meeting with the Board of Oral Research tomorrow and I don't want anything to go wrong. I think we've had enough mistakes lately! (*looks meaningfully at Cornelius*)

Cornelius No of course not, Professor. Will you be taking the animals to the meeting?

Professor (*snaps*) Of course I'll take the guinea pigs. The board will want proof. Though I suppose I'd better take the CD as well. You never know with those wretched guinea pigs. If they refuse to speak I can at least let the board listen to the recordings of the creatures.

Cornelius Of course, Professor. Goodnight, Professor.

Professor Goodnight, Cornelius. (*She leaves. Cornelius busies himself for a while checking the cages and tidying the notes then he too leaves.*)

Delilah (*whispers*) Did you hear all that?

Simon Thank goodness you didn't tell them about our eyesight. My vision has improved enormously after only a few days. It's incredible.

Bernard We should go. We have a long journey ahead of us and we ought to get going.

Delilah (*holds up a paw*) Not yet! (*listens intently*) He's coming back! Lie down everyone! (*The guinea pigs lie down and pretend to be asleep. The door to the laboratory opens and Cornelius re-enters, muttering under his breath.*)

Cornelius Now where did I put my glasses. I'm sure I had them with me a while ago. Maybe I dropped them in the filing cabinet. (*He opens it up.*) Yes of course! Here they are. Silly me. (*Closes filing cabinet and leaves*)

Delilah Right! Let's get going. Bernard, remove the sawdust and get on with gnawing the bars. They only need a couple more bites. Marcia, keep watching the door in case Cornelius comes back.

Simon It's eleven o'clock, everyone. We've got one hour before the night watchman comes around and then we have to be out of here.

Delilah Don't worry, Simon, our teeth have strengthened too – we'll be through the bars in no time. (*The bars snap and the guinea pigs push through the gap and make their way along the shelf. Half way along the shelf they are stopped by a grey rabbit.*)

Rabbit I say, Delilah, will you take me with you?

Delilah (*surprised*) I had no idea you could talk.

Rabbit The name's Sam. They've been giving me the same formula as you, only treble the dose. When I heard you talk of escape I thought I'd like to come. I've gnawed through the bars at the back of the cage. (*The rabbit quickly leaves his cage.*) How are you planning to get out?

Marcia We know the code to the door. We're going out of the main entrance.

Sam (*shaking his head*) That's a bad idea. They've been having trouble with animal activists lately; I heard the security guards talking. (*The guinea pigs look surprised.*) They'll be on the alert.

Simon But that's incredible! Your hearing has developed even more than ours. Those guards are at the front door, far away from here.

Sam Apparently our 'friend' the professor had her car sprayed with red paint the other day by the activists. They really hate her research. The security guards are taking no chances. We have a better chance of escaping through the window.

Delilah But it's barred.

Sam I know it is, but if I'm not mistaken, old Cornelius has forgotten to shut it again. We can squeeze between the bars. There's a ledge outside which leads to the drainpipes. We can slide down the pipes.

Bernard I'm not sure I'll be able to climb along that ledge. I don't really like heights.

Delilah But you managed just now, climbing along the shelf.

Bernard Yes, but I had my eyes shut and held onto Marcia's tail.

Marcia It's true, Delilah, he doesn't like heights. But don't worry, Bernard, I'll help you. Just hold on to my tail again and shut your eyes. I'll guide you down.

Bernard Thanks, Marcia.

Brilliant Activities for Reading Comprehension, Year 6

Sam	Come on everyone. Time's pressing on!

(Suddenly a huge, black rat jumps down in front of them. It has a mean expression.)

Rat	You're not going anywhere unless you take me too.
Sam	(*horrified*) We can't take him; he's one of the virus rats!
Marcia	(*frightened*) Virus? What virus?
Simon	The rats are given two different formulas. One of them is like ours – it makes them bigger, stronger and gives them the ability to speak and read, just like us. The other formula contains a virus, which is lethal to all other animals except rats. Why do you think their cages have been kept away from ours! Do you remember Mavis? They put her in the rats' cage and she got sick … very sick … She didn't make it. The rat can't come with us. He'll kill us. We've already spent too much time with him.
Sam	(*urgently*) Go on, get out. I'll keep him here. (*He glares at the rat.*)

(Delilah looks at Sam, who nods at her. The guinea pigs run swiftly to the window and squeeze through. Sam and the rat circle each other …)

Questions

Answer the following questions with a full sentence:

1. What animals are involved in the escape?

2. Who is the guinea pigs' leader?

3. Why is Professor Patek anxious that all her things are locked away?

4. What special abilities do the guinea pigs have and how has this been achieved?

5. How did the guinea pigs plan to escape and how do they actually escape?

6. Why does Sam suggest an alternative method of escape?

7. Why is Bernard worried about escaping through the window?

8. Why are there security guards at the door?

9. Why do the guinea pigs not want the rat to join them in their escape?

Extension work

1. What do we learn about Marcia from the passage?

2. What do you think Sam is proposing to do in order to help the guinea pigs escape?

3. What do you think will happen next in the play?

4. Can you think of something else the animals might have done in order to escape?

5. What are animal activists and why do you think they have targeted Professor Patek?

6. What reason is given for taking the animals to the meeting?

7. We learn that the guinea pigs have developed further, explain how.

8. How will the CD be beneficial to Professor Patek?

9. In what ways do you think the guinea pigs' special abilities will assist them in their escape and forthcoming journey?

Word work

Give the meaning of the following words:

microscope
vision
alert
lethal
security guard

Brilliant Activities for Reading Comprehension, Year 6
© Charlotte Makhlouf and Brilliant Publications Limited

Goblin Falls

crossing Goblin Falls. Everyone who tries is swept away by the water. I won't do it.'

'Enough!' snapped Hawkcatcher, silencing Lyle with a look. 'You let your emotions run away with you, child. There is a way across the Falls, as the goblins know. Have you forgotten Grace?' Lyle controlled the frantic beating of his heart and tried to focus. For a brief moment 'Grace' meant nothing to him. Panic left no room for memory. Then as panic subsided, memory returned.

'The Goblin Girl,' he muttered, visions of a dark, grinning face appearing in his mind's eye.

Hawkcatcher nodded. 'Grace will help you. She owes me a favour. Rest assured, Grace will help you.'

Lyle did not feel reassured at all. The very thought of the treacherous waterfall made his legs tremble.

Hawkcatcher continued. 'Bypassing Goblin Falls and going around Grimlock Mountain would add days to your journey, days we cannot afford. The company must be stopped and brought back to the castle. Unless we get a message to them, Queen Ling-Su will be

Lyle stared at Hawkcatcher in horror. What she was asking was totally out of the question.

'I can't cross Goblin Falls!' He shuddered. 'It's impossible!'

'You must,' answered Hawkcatcher. 'No other route will take you quickly enough to the Red Road. Queen Ling-Su and her company must be stopped before they come within sight of Lord Garth's people.'

Lyle's eyes were wide as he answered, 'But no one succeeds in captured, and that will surely lead to war. Tens of thousands of innocent people and creatures will die and the land will fall into ruin. You must find the courage to cross the Falls.'

'Why me?' Fear edged Lyle's voice. Hawkcatcher heard the boy's terror and her face softened slightly.

'Because a servant boy will not be missed and I am needed here to put other plans into operation.'

Lyle remained silent. He wished he had never overheard that conversation in the castle cellars. He would not have, if he hadn't been sent to fetch up wine for Lord Garth's feast. Deep in the heart of the castle he heard whispering voices that turned his blood to water. It was Lord Garth himself, and his henchman, Ruskin, discussing an ambush on the Red Road and the capture of Queen Ling-Su.

Lyle had always felt that Lord Garth was an evil man. His face was mean and his narrow, shifty eyes glimmered with malice. Lyle listened as the men plotted to overthrow the throne and seize power.

Lyle scarcely dared breathe lest the men hear him. Finally, the whispering voices moved away. Only then did he slip from his place of concealment and run to the one person he trusted … Hawkcatcher.

'What makes you think that the Queen will listen to me?' asked Lyle.

Hawkcatcher's eyes fixed him with a piercing look. 'The Queen will listen when you present her with this.' She handed Lyle a ring. At first glance it seemed plain but, when held in the palm, its stone glowed with a strange, fiery light. 'She will know the ring and the message it brings her,' Hawkcatcher explained. 'And now it is time to go, for the Goblin Girl will be hard to find and time is running out.'

'Supposing the Goblin Girl will not listen to me? What then?'

'She will come. Just tell her that Hawkcatcher wants a return of the favour. There is no need for explanation. The Girl will understand. Now go.'

Brilliant Activities for Reading Comprehension, Year 6
© Charlotte Makhlouf and Brilliant Publications Limited

Questions

Answer the following questions with a full sentence:

1. Why is it so important that Lyle crosses the Goblin Falls?

2. What might happen if he doesn't?

3. Why does Hawkcatcher say it must be Lyle that goes to find the Queen, and no one else?

4. What does the passage suggest that Grace looks like?

5. Why was Lyle in the cellars and what did he hear there?

6. What does the passage tell us about Hawkcatcher's character?

7. How does the writer convey a sense of urgency in the passage?

Word work

Give the meaning of the following words:

shuddered
subsided
henchman
malice
seize
concealment

Extension work

1. Why do you think Hawkcatcher sends a ring to the Queen?

2. Imagine: who is the Goblin Girl and why will she help Lyle and Hawkcatcher?

3. Do you think Hawkcatcher is right to send Lyle out on such a dangerous journey?

4. Which character do you like the best and why?

5. Why do you think Lyle wishes he had not heard the conversation in the cellars?

6. Of all the threats likely to happen should the Queen be captured, which do you think is the most severe and why?

7. We are told that the conversation was overheard in the cellars. Why do you think this particular location was chosen?

8. Hawkcatcher's face *'softened slightly'*. What does this tell you about her character?

The Journey

It was probably the most boring train journey Chan had ever had.

Some time in the early morning she had left a cold, bleak London. The platform had been filled with shivering passengers, all braced against a spiteful wind that howled down the platform and whipped one lady's skirt up in front of her. Chan would have found the scene funny if she had not been so nervous about travelling by herself to Wales.

'Granny will meet you,' her father had told her, wrapping her woollen scarf tightly about her neck and giving her forehead a kiss. 'It won't be for long. Just until Mum and I sort the new flat out.'

Chan had not really wanted to move from the cosy house, but Dad's job was in trouble and they needed to save money, so they had to move. Chan knew she'd miss the garden. The new flat would not be anywhere as large as the house. Dad had called it downsizing. Mum had said nothing at all. Chan knew that Mum didn't want to move either but there was little she could do about it.

'Can't I stay and help?' she had pleaded, but Dad had shook his head.

'You just have a good time with Granny while we sort out the mess.'

Now she was stuck on the train with little to do and no one to talk to. At first the two seats opposite her had been filled. There had been a cheerful woman with a bright, red coat, who smiled pleasantly at Chan and asked her if she was

travelling alone. She had invited Chan to play cards with her and for an hour they had played Patience and Snap. But then the lady had gathered up her things and said goodbye. The guard had smiled at her when he came down the aisle to check tickets. That was nice of him.

At Birmingham the man sitting opposite her had finally got off, much to Chan's relief and she had been left alone at her table. He had been engrossed in his newspaper and had scarcely glanced at Chan or the red-coated woman.

Brilliant Activities for Reading Comprehension, Year 6
© *Charlotte Makhlouf and Brilliant Publications Limited*

Chan put down the book she was reading and stared miserably out of the window at the leaden sky. The sky had become darker the further the train had travelled. Soon it would be quite dark. Chan reasoned that she must be nearing her destination. She sighed. If only Granny did not live quite so far away. Conwy seemed like the other end of the world and she would be miles away from Mum and Dad. At the thought of her parents, tears prickled her eyes and began trickling down her face. It was as if the sky sensed her distress for at that exact moment, the rain splattered out of the sky and dashed down the dirty windows of the train. Fat raindrops coursed down the thick glass in unsteady rivulets and somewhere in the distance, behind the looming hills, a flash of lightning lit up the sky for a brief moment before retreating.

Chan wiped her face surreptitiously with the back of her hand and hoped the other passengers had not seen her. If they noticed she had been crying they might ask what was wrong and she didn't want to start explaining. But no one seemed interested. They were all engrossed in their books or computers or asleep.

She looked out at the wet landscape. Doubtless it would be just as grey and miserable at Granny's and she would be forced to stay indoors playing endless board games instead of roaming the fields and beaches near Granny's house.

The train slowed slightly and outside the window fields gave way to houses. Chan saw that they were coming into another station. The train shuddered to a halt and a couple of people alighted. Three people entered Chan's carriage. There was something about them that drew Chan's attention. They were an elderly couple and a young man. The couple both had walking sticks and the young man was helping them with their luggage. The old man kept patting the woman's hand and telling her that it would be all right. Chan wondered what would be all right?

The young man was very different. His cropped, brown hair stood up in spiky lengths, their tips a vibrant orange. Chan noted the orange tips with surprise. They went with the long, flamboyant coat he wore. It was the kind of coat a magician might wear, full-skirted and edged with cinnamon velvet. Wonderful colours swirled down the front and on the collar tiny threads of gold had been woven around glinting glass circles. Chan found herself staring at the young man until his gaze met hers. A pair of twinkling, brown eyes smiled into her face and her face creased in response. To her astonishment he sat beside her. All at once, the greyness left the carriage and a steady warmth seemed to fill every nook and cranny. The despair that had clutched her for most of the journey dissolved gently and a feeling of hope lifted her spirits.

'My name is Luke,' said the young man.

Questions

Answer the following questions with a full sentence:

1. Where is Chan going and why?
2. How does Chan feel about going?
3. What different entertainments do the passengers employ on the journey?
4. What do you learn about Chan from the passage?
5. Why do you think that the writer has chosen grey, wet weather as the accompaniment to Chan's journey?
6. Why is Chan reluctant to let people see her cry?
7. Outwardly, what makes the young man different from other young men?

Word work

1. Give the meaning of the following words:

   bleak
   engrossed
   leaden sky
   distress
   rivulets
   surreptitiously

2. If you are 'downsizing', what are you doing?

Extension work

1. What do you think is the central theme of the passage?
2. Imagine you have been on a long journey, describe what it was like and how you felt.
3. Imagine: why does the old man keep patting the woman's hand?
4. Imagine: who or what is the young man with the spiky hair?
5. Describe what happens next in the story.
6. In what way is Chan experiencing an emotional journey as well as a physical journey?
7. Why do you think Chan was relieved when the man with the newspaper left?
8. Find two words or phrases that imply Chan will miss her parents.

The Organisation

'You are late!' intoned The Voice. Olga Popoff slunk into the meeting room, her face crimson. She slithered into the only empty chair. None of the other six people round the table made eye contact with her. None dared.

'I apologise,' Olga stuttered, fumbling with the catch of her briefcase.

'Enough!' snapped The Voice. 'You are here at last. Perhaps now we can begin.'

Olga glanced around the room furtively. The man they knew as The Voice was nowhere to be seen. None of them had seen him or even knew what he looked like. He had always been an invisible presence, though a real and frightening one. He had the power of life and death over them all.

'To business,' said The Voice. Olga could hear the menace in his tones. She sank lower into her leather chair as though to hide. But this was impossible. The Voice could see and hear everything in this sterile, white room.

'There is a traitor in our midst,' announced The Voice.

Olga's heart began to pound in her chest.

'Yes, a traitor. One of you has sent a message using cut-up pieces of *The Times* newspaper when I said the *Daily Mail* was to be used.'

Olga's mouth went completely dry and her brain whirled frantically. Was it her? Had she used *The Times*? She could barely remember. So much had happened over the last few weeks it was hard enough remembering what she had eaten for lunch the day before!

'The Federation of Assassins and Terrorists will not tolerate incompetence,' The Voice continued. 'The penalty is elimination.' Without warning, a flood of some white sticky substance poured down from the ceiling, covering the man they knew as Agent Dahlia. The sticky stuff enveloped him completely. Dahlia floundered briefly and then lay still. Olga felt relief wash over her. Relief that it was not her being punished. She felt little for the man whose life had been snuffed out like a candle. Olga watched as Dahlia's chair disappeared through a trapdoor in the floor beneath where he had been sitting.

'To business,' ordered The Voice. 'Your report, Agent Hollyhock.'

Olga winced. She wished that The Voice had not stipulated they be given flower names. Cars would have been better; she might then have been known as Ferrari instead of Primrose.

Hollyhock shuffled her papers together nervously. Olga could see her hands shaking slightly. They had all been unnerved by the Dahlia incident. Hollyhock arranged her glasses neatly on the edge of her nose and cleared her throat.

'I am pleased to announce that business has been brisk,' she told the assembled company. Three people have asked for our services and all have paid immediately.'

'What about Mrs Kan?' asked The Voice.

Hollyhock looked warily around the room. 'What about Mrs Kan?' she enquired, tension edging into her voice.

'Have you dealt with her?'

Hollyhock gulped and took a quick drink of water. 'It has not been possible to deal with Mrs Kan,' she admitted.

'Explain,' demanded The Voice. 'I do not see why we cannot get rid of a 98-year-old woman. She is far too dangerous to live. We know that she has some idea of Operation Winkle. If she tells the authorities what she has learnt, Operation Winkle will be ruined and our organisation be seriously jeopardised. Why have you not dealt with her?'

Olga glanced at Hollyhock, who was sweating profusely. Huge droplets of sweat were dripping down the sides of her face.

Hollyhock mopped her brow and licked her lips. 'She seems to have

special powers,' she almost whispered.

The room fell silent. 'Explain yourself,' intoned The Voice.

Hollyhock fumbled in her briefcase and brought out a small disk. 'I thought some visual evidence might explain things better than words.'

'Simon,' ordered The Voice. A tall, thin man strode forwards and put out a hand. Hollyhock handed the disc to him. There was a tense silence as they waited for him to insert the disc into a machine. A screen dropped down from the ceiling and the room lights dimmed. On the screen appeared a blurred picture. The recording was not a good one. Olga felt a twinge of sympathy. She knew the difficulties of using a tiny camcorder hidden in a carrier bag with a hole in it. The method had drawbacks, as the recording now revealed.

The screen now cleared and an old woman came into view, gripping a small black handbag tightly to her chest. For someone evidently advanced in years, she appeared sprightly and agile. As she approached the corner of the street a couple of rough-looking boys appeared and advanced menacingly towards her.

'Come on, Grandma,' taunted one of the boys, 'give us yer handbag!'

The old woman appeared unconcerned. 'Why should I?' she retorted. 'It's my bag!'

The young men laughed unpleasantly.

Brilliant Activities for Reading Comprehension, Year 6
© Charlotte Makhlouf and Brilliant Publications Limited

man was lifted off the ground and flung backwards into the middle of the road. His companion stood there disbelievingly, his mouth wide open with shock.

'Now let that be a lesson to you,' she snapped. 'Go away before I call the police.'

The video came to an abrupt halt. 'I see,' said The Voice eventually. 'It would indeed appear that the old woman is possessed of powers. This changes things. She might be of use to us. Agent Primrose,' he barked.

One of them spat into the gutter and cracked his knuckles meaningfully. 'Come on, Grandma, don't be silly. Just give us the bag!'

'Grandma' eyed them disapprovingly. 'I would advise you to stand back if I were you, young man. I really do not wish to hurt you.'

Olga and her colleagues winced as a flood of unpleasant words came from the youths. They cavorted around the woman, shouting and yelling. When the larger of the two tried to snatch her bag from her, she raised a hand and pointed a finger at him. The young

Olga almost jumped out of her seat in surprise. 'Yes, sir,' she stuttered.

'Liaise with Agent Hollyhock. Find Mrs Kan and bring her here at once.'

Olga gulped uneasily. 'But supposing she will not come.'

The Voice laughed unexpectedly. 'She will come. Tell her that Bonzo Collins would be most interested to meet her again.'

Questions

Answer the following questions with a full sentence:

1. Why do you think no one made eye contact with Olga Popoff when she entered the room?

2. Who is *'the traitor'* and what crime have they committed according to The Voice?

3. Why is Olga not keen on her agent's name? What would she rather be called?

4. What seems to be the purpose behind the organisation called the Federation of Assassins and Terrorists?

5. Why does The Voice wish to *'eliminate'* the old woman, Mrs Kan?

6. What special power or powers does Mrs Kan seem to show in the video the agents watch?

7. Briefly describe the room the agents are in.

8. *'I thought some visual evidence might explain things better than words.'* Why does Agent Hollyhock want to show the company visual evidence of Mrs Kan's powers?

Word work

Give the meaning of the following words:

slithered
traitor
incompetence
elimination
profusely
cavorted
jeopardised

Extension work

1. Why do you think The Voice chooses not to be seen?

2. What do you think makes Olga uneasy when The Voice says *'Liaise with Agent Hollyhock. Find Mrs Kan and bring her here at once'* ?

3. Imagine: describe Mrs Kan's other special powers.

4. Imagine you are Mrs Kan. Describe how you felt when the boys came round the corner and confronted you.

5. Olga is the only person who sympathises with Hollyhock. Describe why this is?

6. There is a *'tense silence'* whilst Simon inserts the disc into the player. Why do you think this is?

7. Which phrase tells us that the boys might resort to physical violence?

Brilliant Activities for Reading Comprehension, Year 6
© Charlotte Makhlouf and Brilliant Publications Limited

The School Outing

Ella Jenkins knew this was going to be a difficult trip when the coach failed to turn up. She peered out of the window, checked her watch and then frowned. Nine thirty. She had booked the coach for quarter to nine. She and the class should have been on their way by now.

'It's very late,' she whispered to Mrs Minenski, who was eyeing Polly and Gary beadily.

'I'm sorry?' whispered back Mrs Minenski, still watching the two children. 'PUT THAT DOWN!' she suddenly bellowed, making Polly, Gary and Ella Jenkins jump. The pot of glue Polly was holding tilted alarmingly. She put it back on the table quickly. Mrs Minenski snatched it up, glaring at them, and put it on a high shelf.

'Little nuisances!' muttered Mrs Minenski, returning to Ella Jenkins' side. 'They were just about to pour glue all over Dani's plaits. What a mess that would have made and how would I have explained it to her mother?' She sighed. 'Now SIT!' she commanded the two children. 'And don't let me catch you doing anything else.'

Polly and Gary sat rigid with shock, while Mrs Minenski joined Ella by the window.

'The coach hasn't arrived and the tour of the Stone Age village at Wendlebury starts in an hour,' Ella began in a low voice, anxious that the parents waiting nearby might hear her and register that there was A PROBLEM.

'You did remember to book it?' asked Mrs Minenski.

Ella Jenkins stiffened. 'Of course I did. The question is, did the office pay the booking fee? I'll go and check.' Composing herself, she forced a smile onto her face and left the hall calmly. Once out of the double doors, she raced down the corridor and up the two flights of stairs to the office where a cheery-faced woman sat, thumping heavily on a computer. She looked up at Ella.

'Hallo. Shouldn't you be gone by now?'

Ella Jenkins felt her heart race. Maisie Gordon was a dear, but she had these terrible memory lapses, and sometimes she did seem – was it unkind to think it? – a bit slow. Had she failed to pay the coach company and so put at risk their whole outing?

'I am sorry to trouble you, Maisie,' she began, 'but the coach hasn't arrived and I was wondering if you could check that it really is booked.'

'Wait and I'll find the booking form.' Ella waited while Maisie hoisted herself from her blue, swivel chair, and turned to a big, grey filing cabinet. She took out the file marked 'Trips' and opened it. It took a while to find the right piece of paper. With painstaking slowness, Maisie turned each page. Ella waited in a fever of impatience. She longed to rip the file out of Miss Gordon's hands and rifle through the sheets herself.

Eventually Maisie looked up. 'The coach requisition form is not here,' she said. 'Oh dear, it looks like the coach is not booked.'

Ella Jenkins turned white. 'But I'm sure I booked it,' she stuttered. 'Can I have a look myself?'

Taking the file from the secretary, she flicked through the file. At last she found the section to do with the Wendlebury trip. She checked each form in turn: a form for ordering the sandwiches, a risk assessment form, a list of children going on the trip, a form outlining where they were going and what the trip was about and YES! Stuck to the form about medical details was the coach requisition form.

'It's here!' she said triumphantly, tugging it out.

Maisie Gordon's face crumpled slightly. 'I thought I had looked,' she said, taking the form. 'I'll ring them to find out what is going on and let you know.'

'Please do,' replied Ella, feeling very relieved. She hurtled back to the hall where the parents were looking slightly twitchy, and the children were beginning to show signs of impatience. She clapped her hands briskly and the children fell silent.

'We have a slight problem,' she informed them all. 'The coach has not turned up yet.'

'Yes, it has!' squeaked a voice from the window. 'It's here! It's just coming to the front door now.'

A few minutes later and 38 excited children, together with eight more sober adults, were settling down in the coach. The driver smiled at Ella as she sat down. 'Sorry I'm late, love. Got a flat tyre just outside the depot.'

Minutes later and the coach was off, rumbling out of the school gates and through the main town. The coach filled with eager voices. As they made their way through the town, Ella began to relax. The bright sunny spring day was perfect for a visit to the Stone Age village.

The coach sped down the dual carriageway and onto the motorway, past towns and villages, nestling snugly in fields of green. For a while Ella Jenkins enjoyed the scenery but after an hour she began to feel nervous. Shouldn't they be there by now? Perhaps the driver was taking them a different way?

'How soon will we be at Wendlebury, do you think?' she asked tentatively.

'Sorry, love?'

'Wendlebury!' repeated Ella. 'How far is it?'

'Wendlebury?' The driver looked puzzled. 'No, love, this coach is booked to go to Manchester.'

Questions

Answer the following questions with a full sentence:

1. Why has the class outing been delayed?

2. Where are the children supposed to be going?

3. Why does Ella Jenkins go to the school office?

4. What does Ella think of Maisie Gordon?

5. How many children are going on the trip?

6. What reason does the coach driver give for the delay?

7. What further problem crops up for Ella Jenkins at the end of the passage?

8. What do you think is the purpose of a requisition form?

9. If you are in a *'fever of impatience,'* what does this mean?

Extension work

1. In your own words, describe either Maisie Gordon or Mrs Minenski.

2. How do we know that Polly is up to mischief?

3. What formal paperwork has Ella completed before the class can go on their trip?

4. Why do you think Ella Jenkins forces a smile on to her face?

5. How do we know that the trip is not taking place in winter?

6. Which phrase tells us that the school is not a rural one?

7. If the coach had completely failed to turn up what problems do you think Ella would have encountered?

Word work

Give the meaning of the following words:

rigid
memory lapses
risk assessment
triumphantly

Brilliant Activities for Reading Comprehension, Year 6

The Viking Raid

Knor heard the boats long before he saw them; there was no mistaking the slap of oars hitting the water and the thud of wood against wood. As he perched on the edge of the cliff, his eyes straining towards the swirling mist, he felt weak from terror. Only months had passed since they had last scourged the land and now they were back, just as the wise woman had predicted. Last time, the blood spilt on the land stayed for weeks afterwards, reminding them of the lives the attackers had ended, the possessions they had stolen and the people they had taken away.

Knor took a deep breath and felt his fear give way to rage. He hated the Vikings. He hated the damage they did. They had split his family apart, burnt his home and taken his five-year-old sister, Thyle, into slavery. Loathing burned him. This time he would be ready; he knew what to do.

He watched as the first boats broke through the mist, their dragon prows skimming the water. Knor stared at the leading boat. Raghelm's flag was flying at the top of the mast. Knor's heart beat faster. It was Raghelm who had stolen his sister and Raghelm who had burnt his village.

'He'll not be taking any more of our land,' thought Knor, wrapping his cloak tightly about him against the cold. There was only one other boat. Knor smiled to himself. Raghelm was growing complacent. He obviously thought resistance would be minimal and that only a handful of men would be needed to quell their village.

Knor gathered up his spear and knife and raced back to the Saxon village. The long, wooden meeting hut was filled with groups of nervous people. In the centre, speaking in low, urgent voices were the wise woman and Filgar, their chief. They both turned at Knor's arrival and the babbling ceased.

'They are here,' Knor announced.

A low murmur filled the hut. Frightened eyes turned towards the wise woman. Few doubted her visions but many had hoped that she would be proved wrong. Her gnarled hands twitched and trembled, while her rheumy eyes stared vacantly towards the single window that faced the sea. Her lips moved soundlessly and Knor knew that she was invoking guidance from an unseen presence. Suddenly, the vacant look left her eyes and she turned abruptly towards Knor. The intensity of her gaze made him flinch.

'She knows what I mean to do,' thought Knor, cold rippling through his body. He tensed, waiting for the wise woman to reveal his plan to the entire company; but she remained silent. She merely inclined her head and made the sign of protection over him.

'Men, get your weapons and make your way to the traps,' ordered Filgar. 'At least this time we are ready for them.' He glared into the shadows at a cringing figure. There was no doubt that the Vikings' speedy return was on account of the vile, skulking creature they had acquired during the last attack: Raghelm's son Ragsson.

The prisoner snarled. 'You will not live,' he shouted furiously. 'My father will slaughter you all. Not a man, woman or child will live to tell the tale of our vengeance.'

Filgar watched him in silence. The gods had been good to give them Ragsson. Filgar smiled grimly. Raghelm was on his way back to rescue his captured son but he would not be thanking that coward for all the information he had revealed to them.

Outside the meeting hut Knor joined the men running to take up their positions in the woods. The women and children had left days ago, heading for the caves up in the hills. Knor had watched his mother and younger brother go with the others. Their parting had been painful, for they had all known that he might not see them again.

In the woods, Knor headed away from the others, along a narrow path that led down to the sea. Just above the beach, he crawled into a thicket of deep gorse. The Vikings had beached their boats and were already crunchy across the shingle, their voices kept low. Knor knew that what he was doing was both foolhardy and dangerous. Maybe he should have followed the men to the traps… . Then Thyle's sweet face flashed before him and his resolve hardened. He had made his plans… .

The Vikings were moving quickly now. He could hear them breathing heavily as they stomped past his hiding place, their swords and shields thumping dully against their padded clothing. The menace in their faces made him shiver and he cowered lower in his hiding place. At last they were gone. He looked out. The beach was quiet now except for the soft lapping of the waves on the shingle. Inching carefully from the gorse, Knor crept to the beach. The two boats looked like enormous dragons, towering over him with their graceful heads. Knor set to work. Jumping into Raghelm's boat, Knor began throwing the oars over the sides. Without oars the Vikings would not be able to row. He then slashed at the sail with his knife, until much of it was in ribbons. Knor then turned to the rudder. Leaning over the back of the boat, he hacked at the rudder with the small axe he kept attached to his belt. The rudder creaked and groaned until it finally snapped and tumbled into the sea with a splash. He would have liked to cause more damage, but time was running out. He turned his attention to the smaller longboat. Could he drag it down to the water?

The Vikings had dragged their boats as far as they could up the beach, but the smaller of the two boats rocked slightly as Knor shoved at it. Heaving and pushing with all his might, Knor tried to drag it down the shore. The heavy vessel refused to budge and Knor was about to give up when a large wave slapped on to the shore, drenching Knor thoroughly. To his astonishment, the smaller boat was wobbling uncertainly. He pushed even harder than before. Another wave rushed up the shore, surging under the smaller boat. To Knor's relief, it was now possible to drag it over the watery sand towards the sea. Without a backward glance he slung his bow and quiver into it and leapt nimbly aboard. The boat was filled with stores and supplies. Dust, dirt and rubbish littered

the bottom. He had no idea how to sail the boat, but sail it he must.

A shout from the shore made him freeze suddenly. Had the Vikings returned so soon? He peeped over the edge of the boat and gasped in astonishment. It was his friend Raggin.

'What are you doing?' demanded Raggin, terror on his face. 'If the Vikings catch you … .'

'I'm going to get Thyle!' called Knor.

Raggin's face went white. 'But the Vikings have her!'

'And I'm going to get her back!'

'But you don't know the way. You'll get lost at sea.'

'Maybe so, but at least I'll have done my best,' replied Knor. The boat drifted aimlessly. If only he knew what to do with her.

'I'll help you,' shouted Raggin. 'My father taught me to sail a boat. Help me in before the boat drifts away.' Knor stretched his hands down to Raggin and hauled with all his might. Raggin tumbled onto the deck beside him, gasping and spluttering. Knor helped him upright and gripped his arm tightly.

'You are a true friend, Raggin,' he said simply. 'Thank you.'

Questions

Answer the following questions with a full sentence:

1. Why does Knor hate the Vikings?

2. Who have the Saxons taken prisoner and how has he been useful to them?

3. What is the plan of Knor's that is mentioned in the passage?

4. Who is Filgar?

5. What do we learn about Ragsson from the passage?

6. In what way has Raghelm become complacent?

7. Knor calls Raggin a *'true friend'*. What does he mean by this?

Word work

Give the meaning of the following words:

predicted
slavery
foolhardy
rudder
nimbly

Extension work

1. Why does the wise woman make the sign of protection over Knor?

2. Why is it important to Knor that he damages Raghelm's boat?

3. How is a sense of urgency conveyed in the passage?

4. What major themes are addressed in the passage? Support your response with examples.

5. Identify two particular sentences which you think are particularly striking and describe the effect they have on you.

6. Why do you think Knor's fear gives way to rage when he thinks of the Vikings?

7. We know that the women and children have already left the village. Give reasons for why you think they have already gone.

8. Which words or phrases tell us that Raghelm will not be lenient with the villagers?

Brilliant Activities for Reading Comprehension, Year 6

© Charlotte Makhlouf and Brilliant Publications Limited

The Snagrond

In the cave on Skullbone Island, Flint and Whelkin huddled, staring out at the frothing sea. The full force of the storm was unleashed around them. Its fury was tearing the heart out of the Island, uprooting palm trees and sending the sand spinning in furious whirlwinds. The rain lashed mercilessly down on the cave while thunder and lightning burst from the heavens and made the whole island tremble. Flint was grateful they had left Turtle Island while they could. The thatched huts on the island would have been no protection against the storm or Scrawkins.

'It won't be much longer, Captain,' shouted Whelkin above the howling of the wind. 'You can see them clouds more clearly now and there's light behind them. As soon as they pass, he'll be here!'

Flint nodded. He knew Scrawkins of old. Scrawkins had no fear of storms. He had sailed countless ships through appalling seas and lived to tell of them. The man positively thrived in storms. He used the elements to his advantage and the wind and rain seemed to embrace him and make him their own.

'Are the men ready?' asked Flint, his eyes watching the skies carefully.

'Aye, Captain,' replied Whelkin, 'they're ready to finish this once and for all, even if their lives be forfeit. 'Tis time that pirate Scrawkins was got rid of.'

'A sail! Captain, a sail!' One of the men pointed to the distant horizon. There the skies had lightened to reveal a tiny speck – surely a sail.

Brilliant Activities for Reading Comprehension, Year 6
© Charlotte Makhlouf and Brilliant Publications Limited

'Scrawkins,' breathed Flint. 'At last!' He clambered upright. The cave had been a godsend. They had found it by chance while searching for wood. It had been both an invaluable lookout post and a haven against the storm. 'You know what to do, Mr Whelkin,' said Flint sternly. 'See that the men do as they are ordered.'

Whelkin nodded, sudden comprehension dawning in his eyes. 'But Captain.'

Flint put up a hand. 'That is an order, Mr Whelkin. You will stay here with the men and see that they carry out my orders. I have other business. The Snagrond must be invoked.'

Whelkin's face paled. 'But you can't do that alone, Captain. 'Tis foolhardy! Take me with you. At least I can help you.'

Flint shook his head. 'I need you here, Whelkin. Our plans must be carried out or this whole enterprise will fail. See that the men do as they are bid.'

The distant sail was growing larger. Flint knew now that he hadn't managed to finish off Scrawkins back in Bloodlust Bay. *The Diamond* may be just a pile of ash, but Scrawkins had laid his hands on another ship. The high wind was now pushing it swiftly towards Skullbone Island. Flint tensed. His men had worked hard to prepare for the attack.

The storm slowly moved away and the skies above them lightened.

Flint watched as Scrawkins came closer and closer. Soon the ship was in the bay below. She dropped anchor and boats were launched onto the choppy water, then rowed to shore.

'Tell Jenks to release the fireballs,' Flint ordered. A thin, young man slipped out of the cave and disappeared into the thick vegetation. Minutes later there was a flash and a BOOM and the ship in the bay erupted in flames. Flint smiled wryly. His gunners had done well. A direct hit. The first burning cannonball was followed by a second and a third. Flint could see the men on the beach looking in dismay at their ship, which was now burning badly.

Flint watched the men on the shore scatter, disappearing into the bushes. He permitted himself a sly smile. 'Release the logs!' he ordered. A couple of men ran out of the cave and turned right. Suddenly there was a thunderous crash and a pile of felled trees tumbled down the hillside. Howls and screams of pain could be heard below them.

Suddenly the air was filled with the sound of musket fire and the smell of acrid smoke. Flint knew his men were keeping the enemy pinned down on the lower part of the hill.

'You'd best do it now while ye've a chance,' Whelkin told his master. 'We've not much time left before they reach this spot. Invoke the Snagrond!'

Flint nodded and took a small, black book from his pocket. Nimbly, he ducked out of the cave and pushed his way through the greenery, keeping well away from the path of the enemy.

Brilliant Activities for Reading Comprehension, Year 6
© Charlotte Makhlouf and Brilliant Publications Limited

He made his way steadily down the hill towards the beach. The gunfire continued but at least the wind and rain had passed.

Taking out his book he began reciting the ancient words. As he spoke, Flint felt a surge of power rush through him. Then, as a scream of rage resounded behind him, he turned – and almost stopped his recital.

It was Scrawkins.

The man's face was black with hatred and in his hand he carried a musket. Scrawkins dropped the musket upon seeing Flint and withdrew his sword from its scabbard. Flint knew the pirate was listening to his words, and would know what he was trying to do.

Scrawkins lunged forwards, but Flint was ready for him and dodged nimbly out of the way. Scrawkins brought his sword crashing down, narrowly missing Flint's shoulder. Flint hurried through the remainder of the invocation, looking up at the heavens as he did so. The sky rumbled deeply and the sea seemed to swell up.

Flint stuffed the book back into his pocket just as Scrawkins lunged once more. Flint withdrew his own sword and parried swiftly. The force of his enemy's blow sent waves of pain up his arm and through his shoulders. Flint gritted his teeth and steadied himself. For several minutes, the two men dodged and twisted. Finally, Flint lunged towards Scrawkins' sword arm but the man was too quick for him. He sidestepped neatly and brought his sword crashing down on Flint's sword. Flint doubled up in pain and crashed on to the sand. Scrawkins threw back his head and laughed wildly.

'Did you think to defeat me?' he shrieked. 'What foolishness to think that you could kill the scourge of the sea.'

Flint looked up weakly, his arm burning with pain. In despair, he realised that his invocation had failed. The Snagrond had not appeared. He watched Scrawkins circle tauntingly and then raise his sword.

Suddenly, there was a rush of air and something swooped past them, knocking Scrawkins to the ground and taking the breath from Flint's body. Two huge wings beat the air above them and a giant beak snapped at the sand. Flint cowered helplessly on the sand.

It was the Snagrond.

Questions

Answer the following questions with a full sentence:

1. Where are Flint and his men waiting?

2. Who or what are they waiting for?

3. Who is Scrawkins?

4. Does Scrawkins like storms?

5. Why does Flint not allow Whelkin to go with him to invoke the Snagrond?

6. Who or what is the Snagrond?

7. Flint says, '*I need you here, Whelkin. Our plans must be carried out … .*' What plans are these?

Word work

Give the meaning of the following words:

invoked
countless
musket
enterprise
scourge

Extension work

1. What do we learn about Flint's character from the passage?

2. Imagine: what magical powers does the Snagrond have?

3. In what way does the weather play an important part in the story?

4. What methods of attack does Flint use against Scrawkins?

5. What reasons are given for leaving Turtle Island?

6. How do we know that storms present no difficulty to Scrawkins?

7. Which words or phrases tell us that fate has helped Flint in the story?

Brilliant Activities for Reading Comprehension, Year 6

© Charlotte Makhlouf and Brilliant Publications Limited

Virus on Space Station

TWOPLUTO DAILY NEWS

DEADLY DISEASE ON TWOPLUTO RHUMBA

TUESDAY 28 MARCH 4008

A NEW DISEASE is killing people on Space Station TwoPluto Rhumba. Doctors now realise that the disease is far more serious than they had initially thought. At present, there is no vaccine, and no guaranteed cure, and the disease is spreading.

Symptoms of the disease are wheezing and constriction of the lungs. Tiny blisters form at the ends of fingers and toes which cause intense irritation. Patients complain of intense burning all over their bodies followed by extreme cold. Shocked by the cold, their bodies pass into coma and – far too often – death.

The government has instituted emergency procedures in order to halt the spread of this unseen killer. Schools are closed and people have been issued with breathing masks. Government scientists are working round the clock to find a vaccine that will protect people who have not yet caught the disease. This is proving to be enormously difficult, as it appears that the bacterium which causes the disease has intelligence and is mutating in order to avoid detection.

The illness was first identified at the holiday centre at Sigfelm Delta Colony. Twelve holiday-makers became ill on Sunday night and died in hospital the next day. Two other holiday-makers and three members of staff from the centre are said to be in a critical condition. A six-year-old boy, whose parents are in intensive care, does not appear to be affected by the illness. Doctors are keen to find out whether he has immunity to the new disease, and are monitoring the boy closely.

The boy's parents are

unable – to back up her claim by sharing her evidence with us, and with the public. The government Minister for Health says there is no cause for alarm, and no reason to think that the space station is under attack.

Travel from Two-Pluto Rhumba to Earth and to all the other space stations has been suspended. This is a great inconvenience for those planning to travel on holiday or business. People wanting to return home to TwoPluto Rhumba from elsewhere will have to postpone their journey until the space station is given the all clear.

The government is monitoring the situation closely but says that it is not expected to improve within the next few weeks. Meanwhile, our hope is placed on one small boy and his doctors.

too ill to be consulted about their son. Doctors are hoping the parents will recover soon as they want to find out more about the child's medical history. Information about his childhood illnesses may hold the key to a vaccine against the deadly disease.

One theory, which the government is playing down, is that the disease was deliberately introduced to TwoPluto Rhumba, with the aim of producing a serious epidemic. Doctor Jasmine Wetherby is a proponent of this conspiracy theory. 'There is strong evidence that the disease-causing organisms were introduced to the holiday centre on purpose, with the aim of killing people,' she told this newspaper. However Doctor Wetherby was unwilling – or

Questions

Answer the following questions with a full sentence:

1. Where did the first people catch this new disease?

2. What makes this disease so alarming?

3. What are the main symptoms of the disease?

4. Why is so much hope being placed on the small boy in hospital?

5. Why has travel from TwoPluto Rhumba to Earth and to all the other space stations been suspended?

6. What theory does Doctor Jasmine Wetherby have about the cause of the disease?

7. Choose two sentences which you feel convey the seriousness of the situation.

Extension work

1. You have been asked to compile a list of emergency procedures for residents of Space Station TwoPluto Rhumba. Give three emergency procedures you think residents should follow.

2. Make up a striking newspaper headline about the disease for a newspaper.

3. Imagine: you are a doctor and you think you have just discovered a cure for the deadly disease. Write your diary entry for today.

4. Write a newspaper article for the Sunday 2nd April edition of *TwoPluto Daily News*. Explain what has happened recently with the disease outbreak.

5. If you could write a different headline for the paper, what would it be?

6. If doctors now realise that the disease is more serious than they thought, what does this tell you about their initial ideas about the disease?

Word work

Give the meaning of the following words:

guaranteed
vaccine
immunity
evidence
critical
mutating
postpone

Answers

A Bad Business (*page 20*)
Questions

1. Joseph Grumbleweed has lost all his money, even his shares in Tumbleweed Industrial. OR Joseph Grumbleweed is ruined.
2. The problem was caused by Joseph investing in Tumbleweed Industrial. OR Joseph put everything he had even the family home into a ridiculous scheme, namely Tumbleweed Industrial and as a result he lost everything.
3. Joseph is fearful of his wife's response because she is going to be furiously angry with him. He is frightened of telling her that he has lost the family home and her prized horses.
4. We learn that Henry Mead is an astute businessman who is calm and confident. He is quite capable of disobeying orders should he feel it is necessary to do so.
5. Henry has saved Lavinia's fortune by misleading her as to where the money was invested. Instead of investing in Tumbleweed Industrial, he invested in a property up in the Alps and in a company called Organics R Us.
6. The property in the Alps has trebled in value due to the addition of two new chairlifts and a large cable car which have made the village into a highly desirable ski resort.
7. I think that Henry was prompted to go against Lavinia's wishes, because being a businessman he realised that Tumbleweed Industrial was not a good investment and he decided to invest elsewhere. He might even have had insider knowledge about how the company was doing.

Word work

1.
Obscure – dark and dim, unexplained, something which is concealed
Flinched – to shrink or draw back from something
Blotched – to make spotted, a dark spot on the skin
Mahogany – reddish brown wood
Wrath – terrible anger

2.
A financial advisor gives advice to people as to what they should do with their money to make it work productively for them.

Extension work

1. An example of a simile is: 'Lavinia's wrath whipped through the family home like a tornado'. In this case it conveys Lavinia's furious anger and how this flooded through the home so that everyone was aware of how angry she was!
2. Tension is built up in the early paragraphs through short, clipped sentences and through brief dialogue. It is also built up in the use of words such as 'hoarsely' and 'gravely' which depict the seriousness of the situation. An example would be: 'Is it all lost?' he asked hoarsely'. OR 'It was a bad business'. OR 'Joseph slumped miserably in his thick leather chair.'
3. (Sentences chosen to describe what is felt to be striking, will vary. There should be a comprehensive reason as to why the individual feels they are striking.)
4. Two sentences which describe Lavinia's bad mood are: 'Lavinia's wrath whipped through the family home like a tornado' and 'Now rage filled her as she surveyed the fields' … OR 'Her face, blotched and tear-stained with grief, hardened suddenly.'
5–7. (Require a personal and creative response with reference to the passage if necessary.)

A Sojourn in Bath (*page 23*)
Questions

1. The relationship of the writer of the letter to the recipient is that of sister.
2. Uncle Stephen suffers from gout.
3. We learn that Uncle Stephen is very independent and does what he likes against doctor's orders. He clearly likes his food because he eats a lot and enjoys discussing the menu each day with the chef.
4. We learn that Julia is curious and excited about being in Bath. From the detail in her letter she enjoys writing and describing what she has seen and who she has met. She is probably quite a gossipy character who enjoys chatting with people. Julia might be quite daring as she is keen to meet the highwayman! She is also quite aware of the plight of others as her reference to the amount of food shows. She is caring and thoughtful as she thinks of the urchins and how to help them.
5. Julia is clearly quite excited about the adventure with the highwayman for she would like to meet him and find out where he hides. This is not something her mother would approve of so she has to ask her sister to keep quiet about this part of her news. The highwayman to her appears dashing and romantic.
6. There are many entertainments available to Julia and her mother namely: card parties, luncheons, picnics, taking a walk to the

town to visit friends or the library, tasting the waters, going along the canal, listening to recitals at the Pump Rooms.

7. Mr Erskine Adams is popular because he is a very eligible young man and extremely wealthy. The young ladies are hoping that he will marry one of them!

Word work

1.

Coachman – the man who drives the coach and assists the passengers during the journey

Urchin – a poor, ragged child of the streets

Highwayman – a masked individual who would hold up travellers on lonely stretches of road and rob them at gun point. They rode horses to make a quick getaway!

Milliner – someone who makes hats

Eligible – to be suitable

2.

The vapours are when a lady succumbed to a fainting fit or swoon having had a shock!

Extension work

1. A distinct style is used for the passage to convey the impression that the letter was written a long time ago, in an era when flowery language was prevalent.

2. (Sentences chosen will vary. There should be a comprehensive reason given as to why the sentences were chosen and why the reader feels that they are striking.)

3. We know that the letter was not written today because the language and style are more ornate and flowery compared with letters today which are perhaps shorter and more colloquial. (Examples will vary, possible choices could be: 'We are come to Bath at last!', '… the journey has been a trial to her.', '… which has quite restored Mama's

health already.', 'I confess I felt slightly …', '… might be prevailed upon … ', 'Your most devoted sister.'

4. Food is an issue in the passage because we are reminded that Uncle Stephen's gout is due to eating the wrong types of food and too much of it. There is also an over-indulgence when it comes to food and much waste, which reminds us of the great poverty of some at the time, namely the ragged children in the streets who are hungry.

5. Julia's sister Fanny has not come to Bath because she is unwell … (there should be more description about why she is unwell and how she came to be unwell.)

6–8. (Require a personal and imaginative response so answers will vary.)

Daisy Randall and the Victoria Line *(page 26)*

Questions

1. Daisy does not regret giving up her job as a secret agent. We are told that she does not miss the excitement and the danger.

2. Daisy enjoys her present life because it is quieter, calmer and more predictable. She enjoys knowing that her routine will be the same every day.

3. It is considered hazardous because there is the danger that you could be bumped by others, crammed into a hot carriage with lots of other people, you might lose your footing and, therefore, fall over or lurch into someone else!

4. Daisy thinks that the man cannot be Harry the Strangler because she had killed him twenty one years' ago; therefore he was already dead.

5. The clues that suggest to Daisy that it might be Harry

the Strangler are: his eyes and a small scar in Harry's hairline, also he is as badly dressed as Harry was all those years ago.

6. Towards the end of the passage, Daisy faces the temptation of going after Harry or carrying on to work and her job and letting Harry go.

7. She deals with this temptation by getting off at her stop and following the exit sign which will take her to the place where she goes to work, however, at the very last minute, she leaps back on to the tube just as the doors close and you realise that her training has kicked in once more.

8. The phrase that tells you that Daisy has made a decision about what to do next is: 'Instinct and her MI6 training kicked in.'

Word work

Lurched – a sudden roll to one side

Flustered – to look worried and unsure about what you are doing

Scar – a mark or line that is caused by an old wound which has healed but left a mark

Intrigue – underhand plot or to plot in an underhand way

Nonchalantly – to be unconcerned or indifferent to what is going on around you

Assignment – a task that you have been asked to do either written or action based

Extension work

1. A secret agent works undercover for the government and is involved in secret operations to find things out all over the world in order to protect important individuals, ordinary people and the country generally. (Accept answers that might give details about their specialist skills or reference to specific fiction characters as an example to show what they

mean.)

2. I think that Daisy remembers Operation Thunderbolt well because it was a tricky case which involved a shoot-out and the death of a lot of people. It may be that Daisy remembers the case well because some of her colleagues were killed though this is not mentioned in the passage and because Harry was particularly ruthless and unpleasant. She might remember it because it involved a beautiful location.

3–7. (Require a personal and creative response so answers will vary.)

8. The writer conveys Daisy's anxiety by short sentences. We are also given details about how she feels inwardly 'her heart was pounding' and what she does in the way of actions that denote tenseness and worry 'Daisy gripped the strap even more tightly.' Daisy also has sudden inward panic questions which she asks herself, 'what on earth was he doing here?'

An Unexpected Visitor (page 29)
Questions

1. Mrs Shah is looking through her binoculars to watch the mound of earth in her garden.
2. She dismisses the fact that it might be moles because the damage is too precise for moles.
3. The mound is likened to a 'miniature volcano'.
4. We know that the garden is important to Mrs Shah because we are told that it has taken her years to get the garden looking beautiful.
5. Some of the garden jobs Mrs Shah does are: pruning, weeding, clipping and feeding.
6. The three clues that tell us Mrs Shah is not a young woman are that she has to shuffle down to the bottom of the garden, she has creaky

knees and her arms are frail.
7. It is difficult to see what the creature is wearing because it is liberally smeared in mud.

Word work
Miniature – very small, something of small proportions
Monitored – keep an eye on
Trebled – to become three times as big
Frail – not strong, quite weak
Jerkin – a little jacket which is close fitting and made of leather

Extension work
1. Six adjectives which enhance the description of characters or events are: (adjectives will vary) beautiful, miniature, focussed, precise, tiny, crumbled, shrill, creaky, glaring.
2. At the beginning of the passage I thought that the mound might have been …
3–4. (Personal response required with reference to the passage where necessary.)
5. We learn that Mrs Shah is a determined lady even though she is elderly. She is dedicated and diligent when it comes to her garden and a very hard worker. We also learn that she is frail and yet quite strong when she has to be and her eyesight is poor.
6–8. (Require an imaginative and personal response.)

Autumn (page 32)
Questions

1. We know this passage is about autumn because it tells us that dying leaves are falling from the trees, there's a coldness in the air and the fields relinquish their might.
2. (Requires a personal response, with reference to the text.)
3. I think the mice are eager because when the storehouses are full there will be plenty of food for them to

eat.
4. I think the 'fruits of the harvest' are all the crops that have been harvested by farmers and people who grow food to eat in their gardens or allotments.
5. (Requires a personal response, with reference to the text.)
6. The main theme the poem deals with is the onset of Autumn. Within this there are other smaller themes of harvest and nature's bounty. There is also a more subtle theme of rest and relaxation for nature itself as the trees prepare for their winter sleep. Another theme is that of hard work, the people who help to make the harvest and then bring it in and the hard work done by all the small animals as they desperately gather in what they will need for the winter months ahead.
7. I think the poet means by the line 'winter's coming glory' that winter is a wonderful, glorious season. When we crown a king we glorify the king, so that author is implying that winter is like a king.

Word work
1.
Heralds – signals that something important is about to happen
Resplendent – attractive and impressive through being very colourful and expensive looking
Barren – not producing any fruit or seed, bleak or lifeless
Sustain – to keep going over a period of time or continuously
2.
'The fields relinquish their might …' means that the crops have been harvested from the fields. Crops are very important to us because we need food to eat, which is why they are mighty.

Extension work
1-6. (Require a personal and

imaginative response.)

7. The style of the poem might be considered rather like a prayer in a church, in which praise and thanks are being given for bounty produced by nature 'we give thanks for the blessed rain'. With all the references to 'we' and 'our' it is as if it is one person who is personally giving thanks for the harvest, perhaps a child (reference to the conkers) or a farmer (reference to the eager mice and the storehouses). There are three stanzas and they vary in length. There are no rhyming couplets. The poem is filled with imagery of creatures making the most of autumn and adjectives that remind of how the weather will now change and become colder. The style is also quite antiquated in places namely: 'their labours would be nought' and yet also slightly Biblical: 'nourish and sustain us.'

Cautionary Verse (page 34)
Questions
1. Sam ate beneath the table, secretly in the garden, in his room, and in the cupboard.
2. From the verse we learn that Sam is an exceptionally greedy boy, who is also rather rude because he does not ask people if he can eat their food.
3. His friend's mother likes cooking.
4. Some words which show that he helped himself without asking are: 'without a single 'bye-your-leave'.
5. The moral of this verse is do not be greedy and overeat and remember to ask permission before you take the food from other people when you are staying at their home.
6. We know that Sam has gone too far with his eating because he swells up and dies.
7. The verse is managed through setting the scene of

Sam's awful habit and where he does it. It then follows on to his visit to his friend's house where the awful stealing incident takes place. The verse ends with Sam's sad demise which is the result of his rash actions. The last two verses are shorter and more contained which sharpens the moral being made.

Word work
1.
Raid – to make a lightning/quick attack on something or someone
Diverse – different
Luscious – absolutely delicious
Scoffed – ate very quickly by cramming into your mouth
Demise – death
2.
A cautionary verse is a verse which has a moral attached to it and it is usually aimed towards naughty children with 'difficult' habits.
3.
I think that this line means that Sam's face was going green because he is about to be sick and he leaves the kitchen very quickly knowing that he is beaten because he cannot eat any more.

Extension work
1. If I could give this poem a title, I would call it … because … .
2. All the pairs of lines rhyme. I think that most of the lines work well because … OR I do not think that these lines work well because … .
3. The part of the poem that I like best is the part when … because … .
4. I think that Sam's parents could … .
5–6. (Require a personal and creative response that is individual, therefore answers will vary.)
7. Humour is an essential part of cautionary verse because without it the poet is unable to write outrageous consequences happening without upsetting or offending

the reader. The moral becomes more relevant and direct if humour is added to the verse. Children also respond better to humour, therefore, if the verse has a moral you want them to really take on board and understand, making it funny will help them to learn the lesson better.

Daisy Randall – The Story Continues (page 37)
Questions
1. The story begins on the tube train.
2. Daisy is following Harry because she believes him to be Harry the Strangler and she has unfinished business to settle with him.
3. Harry has not changed much since their last meeting except that he is older and more grizzled and he has acquired another scar.
4. The job Harry is planning is the burglary of Buckingham Palace.
5. The River Thames is going to play an important part because they are going to ship out all the stolen items on a boat via the Thames.
6. When Daisy learns about the job her immediate reaction is laughter because she finds the whole idea absurd.
7. From the passage, we learn that Harry is quick and clever. He has also got very strong hands and unpleasant breath! We learn from Daisy that he is a 'nasty man'. He also has shifty, furtive eyes. From the nature of his plan we also learn that Harry is probably slightly mad and very unrealistic if he thinks he can rob Buckingham Palace. He also has a high opinion of himself as he feels that his plan is 'brilliant' and 'cunning'.
8. We learn that Daisy is calm and resourceful. She has not forgotten her training and applies it to Harry. She is

also slightly impulsive as she ignores the warning voice in her head. When faced with a ruthless person, Daisy is without compassion. Daisy also appears to be sensible and calm when she calls for backup. Her laughter goads Harry into revealing more than he should. At the time this might not be her intention but it works.

9. The Colonel is angry with Daisy for using this particular telephone line because it is a special MI6 line for current operatives. Daisy is no longer a current operative therefore she should not be using it.

Word work
1.
Abrupt – to stop sharply, to be blunt when saying something
Throng – a mass of people all gathered together
Nonchalance – to seemingly be uncaring
Winced – to flinch
Flurry – a slight squall or gust of wind, in this case a bustle of activity as people moved around swiftly
Cronies – old friends
2.
Without compassion means that you are without sympathy for someone.
3.
If something is foolproof it means that it cannot possibly fail.

Extension work
1. The writer predominately uses dialogue within the passage, to give the impression that the action is fast moving and to ensure that the pace of the story is fast and not slow. In this case the dialogue makes it more exciting and the characters' personality shines forth better.
2. Mood is conveyed through the way in which the characters say something, for example: 'he snarled'. Mood is also conveyed through questions

such as: 'How on earth would he and his cronies burgle Buckingham Palace?' It makes the reader curious as to how this can be done and creates tension. Mood is created by the short descriptive sentences such as: 'Up on the street Harry quickened his pace'. Mood is also created by the dialogue between the characters such as: 'They'll kill me if I tell you!' and 'I shall kill you if you don't!'

3. Daisy copes with the challenges of her situation very well in view of the fact that she has not been a secret service operative for a long time. She remembers her training very well up to the point when Harry tries to strangle her and then she regains it smoothly by using her briefcase to hit him! She has remembered many of the moves she used to use to defend herself and this gives her time to sensibly call for backup.

4. If I were Daisy I would … because … .

5. (Personal response required for this question.)

6. I think that there are two possible ways of looking at Harry's claim that the Queen is going to help him. It could be that he is telling the truth and the Queen may very well be helping him or it could show that Harry is completely mad and is under the delusion that the Queen is going to be helping him.

7. (Personal response required.)

Feral Cats *(page 41)*
Questions
1. The story is being told by Patch.
2. Juniper and Patch are concerned when they hear that Pancho has 'crossed the line' because he has crossed over into another gang's territory and that could lead to

a fight.

3. Shadow has the ability to read the thoughts of others and respond accordingly. This could be useful because it will tell her what the other cats are thinking and will give her the knowledge of how to react to them swiftly to deflect a difficult situation.

4. Scar is aggressive towards Shadow because he knows that they are now in danger and because he is keen to be the leader instead of Shadow so he is asserting himself.

5. White Paws is the leader of the Fangs Gang and the brother of Pancho.

6. Shadow has sent Pancho to White Paws to negotiate her marriage.

7. Shadow knows that White Paws will not kill Pancho because they are brothers.

8. We know that the cats are sleeping rough because we are told that they live in a crumbling outhouse and the grass is overgrown. They also sleep among old rags and disused carpet.

Word work
1.
Wary – careful and unsure, watchful
Territory – your land, the area of land that belongs to a particular group
Usurp – to take over a piece of land often by force
2.
A feral cat is a wild cat that has not been domesticated.
3.
Scar says, 'if it comes to war it will be because of his stupidity,' this means that he feels that Pancho's actions were careless and stupid and as a result of them he may jettison them all into a pointless war that could have been avoided had he been careful.
4.
An emissary is someone who goes to give news or advice on behalf of another. In this case, Pancho

is going to negotiate Shadow's marriage with the leader of the Fangs Gang.

Extension work
1. The two sentences I feel are very significant to the story are … because … .
2. I think that Shadow left the comfort of her home to become feral because … .
3. I feel sympathy for … because … .
4. I think that the most important characters in the story are … because… .
5. I do/do not think that Pancho should have kept his relationship with White Paws a secret because … .
6–8. (Require a personal and imaginative response so answers will vary.)

Game Ranger Diaries *(page 44)*
Questions
1. I think that one of the game rangers is writing the diary.
2. I think that the writer is disappointed by the death of the cubs because they had only just been introduced to the pride and they were doing well.
3. A pride takeover is when another male lion or lions attack an existing pride and drive out the dominant male or males. They then kill all the cubs ready to make the pride their own.
4. We know that the lions mean a lot to the writer of the diary because a lot of information is given about them. The person is clearly very sad about the death of the cubs and the state of Ramu. The writer is pleased that Akira and her cubs are safe and well.
5. I think that there have been no diary entries for this period of time because there has been no time to write as the rangers have been too busy looking after the Grundels and other clients and with looking after

Ramu who has been found.
6. Mr Lewis is visiting the reserve to go hunting.
7. Ralph is concerned about Mr Lewis because he does not know how to load a gun and he cannot shoot straight.
8. The lodge has been improved by the addition of new suites which have been finished to a very high standard. They have their own viewing platforms over the reserve and a dip pool.

Word work
1.
Inept – absurd, clumsy
Gash – a deep wound
Dense – thick covering of scrub or bush which makes it difficult to see and move through
Sanctuary – a safe haven
2.
To let nature take its course means that the vet hopes that the animal will die of natural causes without the intervention of medicine.

Extension work
1. The diary entry I find the most interesting is … because … .
2. I think that the writer and Ralph should … .
3. I think that the … .
4–6. (Require an imaginative and creative response so answers will vary.)

Stately Homes *(page 47)*
Questions
1. The Stately Homes magazine comes out monthly.
2. A stately home is a place of historical interest that belonged to someone who lived in the past and is now dead. Their home or place of interest is opened to the public who look at all the things inside from a bygone age. It is a home that is usually beautiful or magnificent in some way.
3. The Bagnum Hall Trust will be paying for the restoration work supported by generous donations from private

individuals.
4. Two topics which are dealt with in this month's issue are Spirits Month and the topic of badgers.
5. Mary Baxter's article is likely to be controversial because badgers are a much loved creature by many people and keeping them under control is likely to generate bad feeling if methods of controlling them are unpleasant. There may be farmers and keen gardeners who are happy to keep them under control as they spread the disease TB in cattle and damage lawns. It could be that there will be a group of people for and against controlling them which is why her article will be controversial.
6. Lord Reginald Actworthy is the owner of Actworthy Hall and he is remembered for the time when he led his servants and peasants against his neighbour Bernard de Courtney who he accused of stealing his sheep.
7. I think that the tickets for the greenhouse are on a first come first served basis because it is only a small space and having large numbers of people in there all at the same time may damage the plants and crops growing there or break the fragile glass of the greenhouse. Also, the constant opening and closing of the doors will let out all the valuable heat!
8. The language for the passage is chatty and inviting. It has a welcoming style to draw readers into the life of the stately homes and to encourage them to visit. There is also an element of advertising in the writing with phrases such as: 'don't forget to…' and 'children are invited to …' and 'would-be Robin Hoods …'. This makes the reader feel welcomed and wanted, especially those with

children. The style is also very positive and vigorous. It starts off with an encouraging 'it has been an exciting …' style that celebrates all the achievements around the country at the different homes.

Word work

1.
Bygone – many years ago, in another era

Haunt – to be followed around by ghosts or to have a ghostly presence in your home

Encounter – to meet with someone by chance

Comprehensive – full and detailed

Falconry – the term given to a sport that involves working with birds of prey some of which are falcons

2.
Bagnum Hall is being restored which means that it is being renovated and the parts that are falling down are being recreated and built again often in the same style and with the same materials.

3.
At the joust people will expect to see knights on horseback using long jousting poles to try and knock each other off their horses.

4.
Concessions benefit people because they mean that people can enter events at a discount and therefore they do not pay as much or they can bring more than one person in with them at a discounted price.

Extension work

1. If I could choose one of the events to go to I would choose the … because … .
2. I think that Stately Homes might appeal to elderly couples who enjoy visiting old and historic homes, or young people with families because there is so much for young children to do and enjoy when they get there and it is often a good way of exploring history. I think that it might appeal to students of history who are

keen to visit different places as part of their courses. I think it could also appeal to nature and garden lovers because many stately homes have beautiful grounds to wander around and enjoy with their dogs and families.

3–6. (Require a creative and personal response which will make answers vary.)

Enquiry into the Danger Zone at Moon Station Gloid *(page 50)*

Questions

1. The enquiry was set up in order to look at the activities within the Danger Zone in response to a fatal accident which happened in the Black Hole.
2. The Black Hole section of the Danger Zone is being looked into.
3. The Danger Zone was designed by Dr Marcia Evans.
4. The purpose of the Danger Zone is to provide a series of challenges for individuals looking for thrilling adventures within a reasonably safe environment.
5. The Black Hole is the most dangerous section of the Danger Zone.
6. If you get into difficulty in the Black Hole section you will be assisted out of the section provided there is no danger to the staff.
7. People entering this section have to cross the Black Hole by means of a rope bridge and try and take an Enzolite crystal which may be hovering overhead. They have to avoid falling from the bridge because there are no safety nets and they will get sucked into the Black Hole.
8. We know that Dougal was not considered to be tired because staff said that he did not appear to be tired, he was also laughing and joking with his friends.
9. We know that he may have

been tired because he had already been in four of the other sections already and it is recommended that you take the Black Hole challenge early in the morning when you are fresh.
10. The rope-haul bridge could present a problem because if you do not have the stamina to cross the bridge then you might drop into the Black Hole beneath as there are no safety nets. There is also no way back across the bridge you have to keep going.

Word work

Logged – written down and noted

Isolated – kept apart from others

Suction – strong pull or sucking in of air

Criteria – reasons given for something to happen, standard of judgement

Extension work

1–7. (Require a personal and creative response. Questions 1–4 need to use the passage for reference and accuracy.)

Marley's Place *(page 53)*

Questions

1. The house once belonged to someone called Marley. He left the house because he said that the quiet depressed him.
2. The house is known as Gargoyle House by the locals due to the ugly lumps of carved stone creatures which jut out beneath the roof.
3. There are three children in the story and their names are Imogen, Sniffy and Jack.
4. The children have been using the house as their special den.
5. The children are reluctant to enter the house because there is a van parked outside it and they do not want to be spotted.
6. I think the leader of the children could be Jack because he is the one who

appears calm and resourceful and he is the one who seems to be making decisions.

7. You learn that Sniffy is very reluctant to enter the house, he wants to go home. You also learn that he has a bad feeling about the situation which tells you he is quite an intuitive child. He is always rubbing his nose with the back of his sleeve and he is quite grubby.

8. Jack is keen to go into the house because he has left the 'stuff' in the attic.

9. The others are reluctant to support him whilst there are people in the house, they don't want to be seen and caught.

Word work
1.
Shrouded – something that is being covered or obscured from sight
Obscured – covered from sight
Encroach – intrude upon something
Cacophony – noise
Vehemently – vigorously and impetuously
Cautiously – to embark upon something with care
2.
This means that the van did not have any logos or signs on the side of it to show which company it might have belonged to.
3.
A self-made man is a man who has made his fortune all by himself. The money does not come from the family wealth or inheritance.

Extension work
1. The opening paragraph is descriptive and atmospheric. It sets the scene clearly and provides a focus for the reader so they know where they are and what time of day it is. There is also something mysterious about the wispy mist contrasting with the beautiful sounds coming from the wood. It contrasts

well with the house because it is as if the house is dead because it is no longer lived in and early mists are compared to the shroud which appears to be covering it, giving it a funereal aspect. The contrast is important because it makes you realise that the children are playing in what is considered to be quite a creepy dwelling. It contrasts with the sweetness and joyfulness of the wood which seems safe and reassuring whilst the house is dark and forbidding and filled with tension and intruders.

2. (Personal response required to this question therefore answers should be atmospheric and evocative with plenty of good description.)

3. I think that the children have hidden … in the attic.

4–6. (Require a personal and creative approach therefore the answers will vary.)

Obituary: Dame Susan Pettigrew
(page 57)
Questions
1. An obituary is a piece of writing that celebrates the achievements of someone who has recently died.

2. Dame Susan was able to spend most of her time travelling because her mother left her part of the fortune she had made.

3. Dame Susan may be considered eccentric because she refused to live in hotel accommodation and lived in her own tent.

4. To help the people in Nepal, Dame Susan helped to set up a small community where women make and sell rugs and the profits are ploughed back into the community for the good of all.

5. Her second book was called 'Rugs of the World' and provides a fascinating insight into the methods of rug

making.

6. I think that women's lives were constrained and dull because they did not have as much freedom as men. They were not able to travel the world freely because it was not considered to be ladylike. Most women were expected to marry, have children and look after a household; they were not expected to indulge themselves in travel.

7. We learn that Dame Susan's parents were special people because they recognised that their daughter needed to be educated and ensured that they gave her the opportunity to learn and travel the world.

Word work
1.
Eccentric – an individual who is whimsical and different from others
Spurned – to cast aside
Cherished – something that is much loved and looked after
Pay tribute – to pay your respects to something or someone
Constrained – limited
Charismatic – larger than life
2.
'I felt as though the world was my oyster' means that she felt that she could do anything, that she had the potential to do a wide range of things.

Extension work
1–6. (Answers will vary as they require an imaginative and personal response.)

Silence *(page 60)*
Questions
1. The poem takes place in the darkening woods.

2. The poet is writing about the time of dusk. We know this because we are told that 'night falls' and the 'darkening woods.'

3. I think that the poem is about … (Accept answers that refer to the way in which night falls and cloaks everything in

peace and quiet and silence. Also accept answers that mention the quietly falling snow that is so silent.)

4. Many different sounds are mentioned in the poem: the sigh of the wind, the rustle of pattering feet, the wind calling.

5. I think that the gloomy shadows might be: animals such as deer drifting into the woods out of sight, or perhaps people trudging through the snow trying to get home. They melt into the tangled undergrowth because they are able to move in and out of the dense undergrowth or in the case of people, they are getting caught up in the undergrowth and are lost and trying to find their way.

6. I think that the pattering feet are the feet of little animals and creatures finding their way through the snow.

Word work
1.
Pattering – the sound that feet make when they move along quickly
Sanctuary – a safe place of refuge
Seeps – when something sinks in
2.
A white wasteland refers to the land covered entirely by smooth snow so that it looks as if nothing is there.

Extension work
1. I think that this is/is not a good name for the poem because … .
2. I would call this poem … because … .
3. The stanza that appeals the most to me is … because … .
4–7. (Answers require a personal and creative response.)

Snegworthy (page 62)
Questions
1. The children are being sent to Snegworthy to get them away from the bombs.
2. Anne is telling the story.
3. The story is told in the first

person which makes it much more personal and filled with personal thoughts and feelings.

4. We know that the children are rather daunted during the journey. Cynthia finds the countryside unfriendly and Lionel is relieved that there will not be any bombs. We know that Cynthia wants her mother and begins to cry for her.

5. Tension is conveyed during the farewell by the dialogue between the mother and the children, in which the mother is desperately fighting back tears and explaining why they have to go and how much she will miss them.

6. We know that Uncle Joe is not totally unsympathetic because he puts the girls in a pretty room with a bedspread that matches the curtains. He has also provided them with a lot of food to eat knowing that they might be hungry after their long journey.

Word work
1.
Dominated – taken control of
Bleak – landscape that is lacking in any features and is very sparse and bare
Loch – large Scottish lake
Craggy – peaks of the mountains that are sharp and dangerous and possibly crumbly
Brusquely – to say something bluntly and briskly without particular emotion
2.
Children sent away from London to safer places were known as evacuees.
3.
An air raid shelter was a place people would go, to take cover from the bombs.

Extension work
1. The war taking place was the Second World War.
2. I think that Uncle Joe … .
3. I think that Uncle Joe says

this to the children because … .

4. I think that Snegworthy is old and untidy and yet clean and comfortable because we are told the bedrooms have pretty bedspreads and are clean. It is a big house and there are lots of rooms which make it secretive and exciting to explore. It is not well cared for as we are told that the windows are dusty. The kitchen is old fashioned compared with a more modern London home because it still has rafters from which pots and pans are hung. There is something gloomy about the house and yet it seems to hide secrets as Uncle Joe tells them not to poke around. I would/would not feel comfortable there because … .

5–6. (Require an imaginative and creative response.)

Song of the Naga (page 66)
Questions
1. A Naga is a type of dragon.
2. The different sounds referred to are the winds that soar over the mountains, the beat of the dragon's wings, the falling pine cones, its great throat rumbling, the heartbeat of the baby dragons, the murmur of their tiny voices as they call through the shells and the song of the Naga itself.
3. From the descriptions the Naga lives in a high inhospitable place where there are woods and mountains. They might also live very close to the waterfall because we are told that the smoke from their nostrils mingles with the watery foam which sounds very close to the nest.
4. We learn that the Naga is a huge dragon because we are told that it has mighty wings.
5. The song of the Naga is the song the dragons are singing to the other Naga dragons

which guides them home.

6.   The phrase I find the most poignant is … because … .

Word work
Words which convey the power of the Naga are: mighty, great, beat.

Extension work
1.   I think you are advised to tread carefully near the great eggs in case you break them or tread on them, or wake them and make the baby dragons call out a warning to their mothers.
2–4.   (Require a creative and personal response so answers will vary.)

Dragon Lore (page 68)
Questions
1.   A Thayle is a type of dragon.
2.   Some people believe that dragons are a myth but in the passage we are told that they 'are as real as the leaves on a tree.'
3.   The hatching and rearing process requires great skill and dedication.
4.   Emerlot Twingbee's book is called *Thayle, Truth and Fantasy*.
5.   The deer helps Emerlot because it disappears into the waterfall. This helps Emerlot to realise that there must be a path through the waterfall.
6.   Emerlot sees a tiny black speck weaving and looping in the sky and this tells him that he has found his Thayles.
7.   Some of Emerlot's feelings are: daunted because he cannot see his way down, he moves cautiously. He is pleased and excited at the thought of finding the path behind the waterfall, he gets to the other side of the bank and feels greatly relieved for having done so. The way to the top is considered 'daunting' by Emerlot. When he sees the Thayles he is so amazed, he stands transfixed.
8.   Another phrase which

describes the waterfall is: 'gushing curtain' or 'fall of water'.

Word work
1.
Myth – a tale with supernatural characters in it
Dedication – investing a lot of time and energy in something
Canyon – a deep gorge
Transfixed – to be astounded such that you are unable to move
Cautiously – carefully
Startled – to be taken unawares
Daunting – to find a situation frightening or difficult
2.
This means that Emerlot stood absolutely still, unable to move because he was so filled with awe as he watched the Thayles swooping and diving in the air.
3.
Well-trodden means that a path has been walked upon a great deal by either people or animals.

Extension work
1.   Understanding came to me in a blinding flash! There had to be a way through the waterfall! OR Suddenly my mind understood what must have happened! There had to be a way through the waterfall! (Other variations may be given).
2.   (Adjectives may vary but an explanation should be given as to why they were chosen and what they mean.)
3–5.   (Require a creative and imaginative response, so answers will vary.)

Stately Phantoms (page 71)
Questions
1.   The writer met Penelope at a musical evening at Rednock Manor.
2.   Penelope was striking because she had flaming auburn hair and she was wearing an elegant black gown.
3.   On the evening in question the writer learnt that Penelope

was a very good artist who had painted a number of pictures at Rednock Manor. She also loves cats.
4.   Later on we learn that Penelope died tragically trying to save her pet Linus from the river. We learn again that she is a talented artist who had a great love of animals especially cats.
5.   The other people at the concert looked puzzled because it must have appeared that Griselda Hall was talking to herself.
6.   Iris Delafield was an American lady who was visiting Toorock Castle.
7.   Iris saw a couple of rowing boats coming to land and six strangely dressed men get out. They were carrying barrels which they deposited in a cave and then left again by boat. When the visitors investigated the cave there were no barrels there at all and it was empty.
8.   Henrietta Williams is an authority on the supernatural. The three specific details she asked for were: What had Penelope been wearing? What was the atmosphere around her like? How did the other guests respond to the writer?

Word work
1.
Naïve – not being very worldly-wise.
Auburn – reddish brown coloured hair
Tragic – very sad and unexpected
Smuggler – someone who would bring contraband goods ashore without the excise men knowing and sell them secretly to locals
Encounter – to meet someone or something often by chance
Headland – the area of land jutting out from a cliff around which boats can sail
2.
A minstrels' gallery is a platform

raised above a room through which people can look down. It is where the small orchestra would sit in olden days when the lord of the manor wanted to be entertained.

3.
A phantom is another word for ghost.

Extension work

1. The words or phrases that tell us that Iris' encounter was peculiar are: 'she had been gone for no more than a few minutes … for over half an hour watching the men' and 'I checked the cave and found no barrels there at all.'

2. Toorock is a popular tourist attraction because it is an impressive castle on the Devon coast and it is known to have been the haunt of smugglers. There is a romantic appeal to it because it is on a rugged cliff surrounded by wild moorland. There are also plenty of ghosts there so many people would be attracted to it in the hope of seeing some of the ghosts.

3–6. (Require a personal and creative response therefore answers will vary.)

7. Arriving by boat at Toorock is considered to be romantic because tourists get the feel of what it must have been like to have been a smuggler arriving secretly at night to the beach.

The Case of the Missing Turtle
(page 74)
Questions

1. The village fête is being held in aid of the Widows and Orphans Benevolent Fund.

2. The real organisers of the fête are Reverend Sally, Miss Hartley and her team of willing helpers.

3. We know that Miss Wimpole is not a young woman because we are told that she would like to look at Mr Simpkins' pictures as it would remind her of her youth and the time she spent there as a young girl.

4. Miss Wimpole has contributed a number of small knitted items to the fête.

5. Sydney is Mr Graves and he has died from a nasty gash on the head.

6. The turtle is special because it is decorated with coloured stones and its back opens to reveal a secret compartment in which earrings may be kept.

7. From their conversation together, we learn that Miss Wimpole and Mr Simpkins know each other well and are good friends. From the way in which Miss Wimpole smiles indulgently at him you get the impression she looks on him fondly like a son or favourite nephew.

8. I think that Miss Wimpole looks through the scattered glass and pottery to see if she can locate the turtle. The fact that she hunts for it tells us that she already has an inkling that it will have disappeared.

9. I think that Miss Hartley stares 'disgustedly' at Sydney because he has inconveniently died in the middle of her fête and ruined it. He had also made a mess of the stall and that has annoyed her considerably when all the ladies took so much time and trouble to make the fête look nice.

10. When he was in Egypt Mr Simpkins had a ride in a felucca, he bought a model pyramid that opened up, he visited the Valley of the Kings and took many photographs.

Word work

Frenzy – when people are bustling about in such a busy way they look out of control

Bric-a-brac – items on a stall of different shapes and sizes and for different purposes, often things that people no longer want at home that have been donated, eg cups and saucers, egg cups, napkins, pictures, ornaments

Quaint – very pretty and nice in an old-fashioned type of way

Reveal – let people know about something

Gash – a deep cut

Extension work

1. I think that Miss Wimpole thinks that the tea tent is 'an excellent position' because it affords her a very good view of everything that is going on at the fête and she can see all the different stalls.

2–7. (Require a personal and imaginative response, so answers will vary.)

8. Children should look at both the passages in depth to compare and contrast the language in each, how they are the same and how they are different. Both are told in the first person, both are quite chatty and informal in style. Some of the language is quite antiquated, for example, the way Mr Simpkins says, 'nothing would give me greater pleasure.' There is something gentlemanly about his manner. The conversations in Stately Phantoms are more modern sounding. There is something very Miss Marpleish about the Case of the Missing Turtle.

The Cookery Competition *(page 77)*
Questions

1. The dishes Denzel will be creating for the competition are a salmon paté garnished with chives, Beef Wellington and a traditional rice pudding.

2. Denzel is feeling under pressure because everyone else is much older than him and so much more confident and poised.

3. The blood drains from Denzel's face when he hears that Henry Tomkinson is one of the judges, because he has

stolen a salmon from Henry Tomkinson's stretch of river.

4. We know that Henry Tomkinson has a very unpleasant temper and that he guards the fish in his river to avoid poachers taking them. If you want to fish in the river you have to pay Henry a lot of money to do so which means he may be quite a venal, greedy man too.

5. We know that Denzel is a little bit of a day dreamer who is keen to win the competition to prove he is a good cook and so that he can learn from another famous chef. He is a hard worker who is also a perfectionist – we know this because he has already practised what he wants to make many times beforehand. He is also creative and inventive because he likes to think of ways of making his dishes attractive and pleasing to the eye as well as the mouth and he grows his own vegetables. Denzel is also rather a risk-taker – by taking the salmon from the river we learn that he is also a poacher!

6. We know that he has worked hard because we are told that he has already made eight Beef Wellingtons beforehand until he was satisfied and we are told that he has practised in his own kitchen for weeks.

7. The possible problems he faces with his Beef Wellington are that it would be easy to overcook it and leave the meat on the inside underdone.

8. We learn that Denzel is quite intimidated by the other competitors because they are confident and poised. He also feels that they are smug and self-satisfied and do not want to talk to him because he is not as important as they are.

Word work

Poised – standing upright and with good posture, holding your body upright with confidence

Self-satisfied – having a very good opinion of yourself

Eulogised – to proclaim something to be almost holy it is so beautiful, in this case, good to eat

Connoisseur – someone with excellent knowledge and experience in a particular field of expertise, eg cookery or wine

Traditional – something that is well established, in this case the rice pudding is a well-known and loved typically English dish that has been around for a very long time

Extension work

1. Tension is conveyed through the thoughts and feelings of Denzel as he watches the other competitors and worries about their abilities compared with his own. It is also conveyed in the way in which Denzel tries hard to focus his mind on what he will be cooking, but there is more tension there as he realises that the Beef Wellington could go wrong and the rice pudding might not be good enough compared with the other competitors who might make their dishes fancier. There is tension when we are presented with the judges and we learn that Henry Tomkinson is one of the judges and all that entails. The writer uses short sentences to convey the tension and description to set the scene in which the fish is stolen which will then heighten the enormity of what Denzel has done and add more tension.

2. I think that the most difficult dish to make will be the … because … .

3. I do/do not feel Denzel was justified in obtaining the fish in the way he did because … .

4–7. (Require a creative and personal response so answers will vary.)

Shopping Centre Opens (page 80)

Questions

1. A shopping complex is an area in which a variety of shops are situated in close proximity to each other to make the shopping experience easier for the shopper.

2. The reason given to justify Happyfields is that it will provide more choice.

3. The initial problems the project faced were opposition by the local people who felt they had enough shops already and the siting of the complex.

4. Ludwig Dunwitch was probably reluctant to discuss the problems because they undoubtedly caused a great deal of bad feeling and arguments and he does not want to have to go into details again and have it logged in the newspapers.

5. The difficulties the shopping centre is likely to face in the future will be whether or not it will survive because many of the shops cater for the very rich only.

6. Happyfields will be a positive contribution because:
   • It has regenerated a piece of old wasteland.
   • It has a huge number of shops for people to wander around
   • Car parking which will give people somewhere to put their car
   • The new cinema will give people more choice
   • Work for local people.

7. It will not be a positive contribution because:
   • The shops are for the affluent only
   • Cinema tickets will be very expensive
   • Too great a contrast as a structure with cottages

nearby
- It will be an eyesore
- Land could have been used for a playground.

Word work

Opposition – to be against something

Vast – very large proportions

Numerous – many

Siting – position of something

Dwarfed – over shadowed by something that is larger

Dubbed – given another name perhaps not a polite name

Affluent – very wealthy

Extension work

1. The choices being offered are the ability to have more shops to choose what you would like to buy, the choice of more films at the cinema. These are probably the only major choices people will have.
2. The future of the Portly Street Cinema is uncertain because the new cinema may take all their business which means they will not be able to stay open.
3. I think that the most challenging problem Happyfields is likely to face is … because … .
4. If I could give Happyfields another name I would call it … because … .

The Dark Side (page 83)
Questions

1. Lucy lived in an orphanage because her mother died when she was a baby and she had never known her father.
2. Macgregor Smythe is the local abattoir man and Lucy was going to be sold to him.
3. Lucy leaves the orphanage by escaping in the laundry truck with Charlie.
4. We know that life on the streets is hard for Lucy because she has to escape from the secret street police, she has to fight for a place to sleep, she has to fight and hunt and pay her money to

the underworld king, she gets her food from dustbins or kindly café owners, and there is every chance she might be attacked by other beggars with a knife.

5. It is dangerous because other beggars also look for food in dustbins and they might not be keen to share their pickings, so Lucy might be attacked.
6. The men with mean hard faces are the secret street police.
7. Lucy met Old Ned when she was on the run from the street police. She raced through some alleyways and came to a dead end. A hand came down from the top of the wall and helped her up and over it. It was Old Ned.
8. I think that Old Ned means that the Dark Side is a place where … (Answers will vary according to what the children think that The Dark Side could be.) He is quick to caution against it because he knows that The Dark Side is evil and will lure Lucy into a world from which she cannot escape and that it might be much worse than the life of beggary she is currently experiencing.
9. Lucy is ten when Old Ned tells her about the Dark Side.

Word work

Abattoir – a place where animals are killed for meat

Orphanage – a place where children with no parents live

Unkempt – of untidy and dishevelled appearance

Infiltrate – to get in somewhere by stealth and cunning

Tantalisingly – to tempt someone through smell or taste

Protector – someone who looks after others

Extension work

1. Suspense is maintained by the brief sentences and short paragraphs. The passage starts with a sentence of

suspense in which we hear about the voices. The fact that Lucy is constantly on the run from the police and that their presence is always there adds suspense. Descriptions of people like Macgregor Smythe add suspense because he is clearly evil. Lucy is often described as on the run or running away, this makes the pace of the passage faster and adds suspense.

2. The part of the passage when … intrigues me the most because … .
3. In order to survive Lucy has learnt to:
   - Be cunning
   - Evade the secret police
   - Be quick-witted and nimble
   - Fight and hunt
   - Pay her money to the underworld king
   - Find food
   - Run quickly and dodge people
   - Learn where the secret places are so she cannot be found.
4. I think that Lucy made the right decision to leave the orphanage because … OR I think that Lucy did not make the right decision to leave the orphanage because … .
5. Two sentences which describe the hopelessness of her situation are: 'terrified, she looked right and left … the street police waited' and 'The cardboard box had been Lucy's bed for a couple of months' and 'Her stomach churned with hunger …' (There are quite a few possible answers which convey the hopelessness of her situation.)
6–8. (Require a personal and creative response.)

Everest (page 87)
Questions

1. Mount Everest is in the Himalaya range of mountains.
2. Hypoxia is caused by a lack of

oxygen to the brain.
3. The symptoms a person with hypoxia show are impaired judgement, they become confused and they do not know where they are and what they are doing. They also go into a trance-like state in which events and objects are magnified out of proportion.
4. Climbers with large lungs might be at an advantage because their lungs can absorb more oxygen.
5. The Khumbu Icefall is hazardous because it is unpredictable. It is filled with deep crevasses and huge ice blocks which can crush you or which you can fall down and when it is hot the icefall becomes more unstable.
6. Climbers are helped across crevasses by fixed ropes and ladders.
7. The Death Zone is located at 26,000 feet on the mountain where the air is thinnest.
8. The Death Zone is given that name because this is the place where the body uses up its store of oxygen very quickly and it cannot be replenished, the muscles begin to waste away and the body becomes weaker.

Word work
1.
Crevasse – an opening in a glacier that is very deep and down which people can fall, a fissure of varying length and depth that can be found on a glacier
Traverse – to cross over something
Glacier – a frozen river of ice that is always moving imperceptibly slowly
Maximum – the most amount of something, eg time
Decrease – to lower or get smaller
2.
If your judgement is impaired it means that you are not making good decisions about what you

should be doing.
3.
If a place is inhospitable, it means that it is not welcoming and friendly.
4.
To become acclimatised means that your body is becoming adjusted to living on the mountain.

Extension work
1–3. (Require a personal and creative response therefore answers will vary.)
4. Shortage of breath and a lack of sleep are troublesome on a mountain because not being able to breathe properly would make it very difficult for you to climb and move around properly whilst the lack of sleep would mean that you would be constantly tired and therefore prone to making careless mistakes that could cost you your life.
5. The great dream that climbers achieve is that of climbing Everest, which is a tremendous achievement. The price they might pay could be death if they don't make it or the loss of fingers and toes due to frostbite. In order to achieve your dream of climbing Everest you might have to sacrifice something in order to get there.
6. The two phrases which best describe how dangerous Everest is are: 'An extended stay in the Death Zone without extra oxygen will end in death.' And 'In 1996 eight people died in a single day on Everest.'
7. I think that the research that has been gathered will help future climbers because they will:
   • understand how the body works better at altitude
   • be able to make better medicines to help climbers who fall ill
   • be able to establish more effective ways for climbers

to acclimatise
   • find ways of monitoring whether climbers are in the early stages of hypoxia.

The Formula Part 1 *(page 90)*
Questions
1. The action takes place in an animal laboratory.
2. Delilah the guinea pig can speak because she has been given something called Dipopsonocum N2134D.
3. Simon has been able to read a book entitled *The Future of the Universe.*
4. We learn from Delilah that the dosage was not the lowest but a whole pipette full. We learn that Cornelius became bored with measuring out such tiny amounts so he simplified the dose. As a result, the animals' intelligence has increased.
5. The Professor needs to be absolutely sure of her facts because she is going to be speaking to the Board of Oral Research about her findings.
6. Delilah is doubtful that the humans will want animals to possess greater intelligence than them and questions where it will leave the humans if animals are more intelligent.

Word work
Furtively – to do something sneakily
Dosage – the amount you give something or someone, something that is carefully measured
Simplified – made more simple or easier to deal with
Converse – to talk with someone

Extension work
1. Stage directions are the bracketed pieces of information that tell an actor where they should go on stage or what they are meant to be doing or how they are feeling.
2. The dosage is important to the Professor because she will need to tell the board exactly

how much of her formula she gave the animals so that if they want to check her work they will know exactly how much to give. The dosage is also important because she has to know exactly how much to give the animals or the results might not be the same.

3. I think that if animals could speak they would have greater power, the ability to tell us how they think and feel, the chance to make decisions for themselves and to tell us how we should be doing things. They would have the power to make decisions about how they want to be treated and whether they should be used for food. (Some children might make an analogy between this and George Orwell's *Animal Farm*.) We might find ourselves in a situation where animals rise up against humans! We also might find ourselves in the situation when the animals gossip to others about personal and private things that happen in our homes!

4. Four guinea pigs are introduced to us altogether: Marcia, Bernard, Simon and Delilah.

5. Delilah speaks to Cornelius as though he is a very naughty, disobedient child. She talks to him as though he is an idiot!

6. The Professor lowers her voice conspiratorially so that other people cannot overhear what she is saying and to preserve the secrecy of her operation. She might also be lowering her voice so that the guinea pig is not aware that she has been overdosed.

7. From the passage we learn that Cornelius is lazy and negligent. When he is caught out, he tries to make excuses and wheedle his way out of trouble.

8. I would rename the passage

… because … .

The Formula Part 2 *(page 93)*
Questions
1. The animals involved in the escape are the guinea pigs and a grey rabbit.
2. The guinea pigs' leader is Delilah.
3. Professor Patek is anxious that all her things are tidied away and locked away, because she does not want anyone stealing all her important research.
4. The special abilities that the guinea pigs have are that they can speak, their eyesight and hearing have also improved considerably. We also learn that their teeth have strengthened too. This has been achieved by giving them a special formula.
5. The guinea pigs are planning to escape by going out through the main entrance. They change this to escaping via the window, going along a ledge and then down the drainpipes.
6. Sam suggests an alternative method of escape because of the animal activists which have alerted the guards at the main door. This means that there will be more guards on duty which means that there is more of a chance that the animals will be spotted.
7. Bernard is worried about escaping through the window because he does not like heights.
8. There are security guards at the door to prevent the animal activists from entering the laboratory and from spray painting the cars.
9. The guinea pigs do not want the rat to join them because he is one of the virus rats and he might give them a virus which will kill them.

Word work
Microscope – a special piece of scientific equipment that

magnifies things and makes them larger
Vision – the ability to see, eyesight
Alert – to be ready for action
Lethal – dangerous enough to kill
Security guard – someone who is in charge of making a place safe

Extension work
1. We learn that Marcia is kind hearted and eager to help her friend Bernard who is frightened of heights.
2. I think that Sam is proposing to risk his own life to help the guinea pigs to escape and to keep the rat from following them.
3–4. (Personal and creative response required for these questions.)
5. Animal activists are people who are against animals being kept in laboratories for testing and they do what they can to cause trouble and to get the animals out of the labs. This is why they have targetted Professor Patek.
6. The animals are being taken to the meeting as proof that they can talk.
7. The guinea pigs have further developed through better hearing, eyesight and stronger teeth!
8. The CD will have recordings on it of her conversations with Delilah and will prove to the board that the guinea pigs can speak.
9. I think that their new special abilities will help them in their escape by … (answers will vary).

Goblin Falls *(page 97)*
Questions
1. It is important that Lyle crosses Goblin Falls in order to get to the Red Road quickly.
2. If Lyle does not cross Goblin Falls Queen Ling-Su will not be stopped and brought back to the castle and that will lead

to war.

3. Hawkcatcher says it must be Lyle because a servant boy will not be missed and Hawkcatcher is needed for other operations.

4. The passage suggests that Grace looks like a naughty elf with her dark, grinning face.

5. Lyle was in the cellars collecting some wine for Lord Garth's feast and it was there that he overheard plans about the ambush on the Red Road.

6. From the passage we learn that the Hawkcatcher is tough and not driven by emotion. We learn that she is decisive and she is a leader. She is also kind because her face softens when she realises that Lyle is frightened.

7. The sense of urgency is conveyed through simple, short sentences and by dialogue which is crisp and terse. The descriptions of Hawkcatcher's face and the consequences of actions convey urgency.

Word work
Shuddered – to involuntarily tremble with unease or worry
Subsided – when something goes down, like a water level dropping
Henchman – someone who works alongside their chief
Malice – to do something unkindly
Seize – to grab hold of or capture something
Concealment – hiding

Extension work
1. I think that the Hawkcatcher sends Lyle with a ring so that the Queen knows that the bearer of the ring is honest and that the message is a truthful one and should be listened to.

2. I think that the Goblin Girl is … because … .

3. I do/do not think that the Hawkcatcher is right to send Lyle because … .

4. The character I like the best is

… because … .

5. I think that Lyle wishes he had not heard the conversation because then he would not have to risk his life crossing Goblin Falls.

6. I think that the most severe threat to the Queen will be the threat of war when thousands of people will die.

7. I think that the location of the cellars was chosen because they are a good deep place far below the main bulk of the castle away from prying eyes and ears where people can be concealed.

8. Her face 'softened slightly'. This tells us that she is a kind person and sensitive to the fact that Lyle is frightened.

The Journey *(page 100)*
Questions
1. Chan is going to Wales to stay with her Granny.

2. Chan does not really want to move to Wales but her Dad's job is in trouble and she knows that they must save money so they have to move.

3. On the journey, the passengers play cards, or read newspapers or books.

4. We learn that Chan is a thoughtful, helpful girl who is sympathetic towards her parents and their difficulties. She is also happy to be by herself and yet able to mix with others should the need arise. She is also observant as there is a lot she takes in when the old couple and young man get on the train.

5. I think that the writer has chosen grey, wet weather to reinforce Chan's sadness at having to move away from home. It is overcast to show her resigned attitude towards leaving and the slight hopelessness she feels at leaving people and things she loves behind. The rain could also symbolise her tears. The weather is also symbolic of

Dad's bleak situation.

6. Chan is reluctant to let people see her cry because she does not want to have to explain to them why she is unhappy and relive the whole situation once again.

7. Outwardly the young man is different from other young men because of his hair and clothes; he is very flamboyant and colourful rather like a magician and most young men do not look like magicians.

Word work
1.
Bleak – without hope
Engrossed – to be focused on something, in this case reading
Leaden sky – a sky that is very grey and overcast
Distress – upset
Rivulets – the way in which water runs down a window in what looks like little rivers
Surreptitiously – furtively, secretly
2.
To downsize is to move to live in a smaller place.

Extension work
1. I think that the central theme of the passage is that of moving house and coming to terms with the idea of downsizing as a result of changing family circumstances. OR I think that the central theme of the passage is a journey in which the train represents Chan's life moving in another direction and the fact that she has to come to terms with this. (Accept other reasonable responses that relate to change and individuality and personal fears and worries.)

2. (Personal response required for this question.)

3. I think that the old man keeps patting the old woman's hand to reassure and comfort her.

4. I think that the young man is

5. (Personal and creative response required for this question.)

6. Chan is experiencing an emotional as well as a physical journey because she has to leave all that she is familiar with behind her in order to go to a new home in a new part of the country. This must be quite traumatic for her because she has to cope with leaving her parents for a short while and she has to travel alone which will allow her to dwell on her situation. She is also not just unhappy on the journey but lonely as well because there is no one to talk to or play with.

7. I think that Chan was glad when the man with the newspaper left because he had not been any company at all, he had just sat and read his newspaper and kept to himself. Chan might have found this quite intimidating especially if he held his newspaper up rather like a barrier between them both. The fact that he leaves would also give her more space to stretch her legs and relax.

8. The two words or phrases that imply Chan will miss her parents are: 'Can't I stay and help?' and 'Chan wiped her face surreptitiously …' and 'Mum and Dad. At the thought of her parents, tears prickled her eyes …' and 'The despair that had clutched her …'.

The Organisation (page 103)
Questions
1. I think that no one made eye contact with Olga Popoff when she entered the room because they were all terrified that by giving her eye contact they were, in some way, giving her support for being late and that in turn would get them into trouble. OR They were frightened of acknowledging her because

she was late and that meant she was in serious trouble and they did not want to be associated with anyone who had done something wrong.

2. The traitor is Agent Dahlia as he dared to send a message using cut-up pieces of The Times newspaper when they were expressly told to use The Daily Mail!

3. Olga is not keen on her agent's name because they are the names of flowers. She probably feels that being given the name of a flower is rather wishy-washy and not very agent-like. She wishes they had been named after cars and then she could be Agent Ferrari rather than Agent Primrose.

4. The purpose of the organisation is to eliminate people for other people.

5. The Voice wishes to eliminate the old woman because she has some idea of Operation Winkle and if she tells the authorities about it then their plans will be ruined and the organisation jeopardised.

6. Mrs Kan has special powers. She has the ability to lift people up off the ground and fling them around or down on to the ground just by raising a finger.

7. The room the agents are in is a meeting room. There are leather chairs for the agents to sit in. Somewhere in the room is a machine for DVD discs and a screen which drops down from the ceiling. The room is sterile and white and somewhere in the ceiling is a mechanism which releases the sticky white stuff that will eliminate traitor agents.

8. Agent Hollyhock wants to show the other agents visual evidence because she feels that if she explains what the old lady does the agents will not believe her, therefore, visual proof will speak louder

than words.

Word work
Slithered – to move like a snake sliding and twisting
Traitor – someone who betrays another
Incompetence – not able to do something with any degree of efficiency or ability
Elimination – to get rid of something or someone
Profusely – a lot, too much
Cavorted – to leap around a great deal
Jeopardised – to put something into danger

Extension work
1. I think that The Voice chooses not to be seen for a variety of reasons; he or she wants to keep his identity secret from the other agents, he or she might be particularly revolting to look at and therefore they might want to hide away because of this.

2. I think that Olga feels uneasy about liaising with Agent Hollyhock because if they fail to bring Mrs Kan in to meet The Voice, they will undoubtedly be punished or eliminated.

3–4. (Personal and creative response required for these questions.)

5. I think that Olga sympathises with Hollyhock because she has had to use surveillance equipment before and found that it is tricky and often unreliable to use. If the picture is blurred and poor then the image she wants to show will not be very visible which might mean that no one will believe her and she will be punished. Also, if she shows that she is not very good at using the equipment and it is poorly filmed she might again be punished.

6. I think that there is a tense silence whilst Simon inserts the disc because they have no idea what to expect from

the information, or it could be deeply unpleasant to look at or they are nervous for Simon because the equipment might not work. If it does not work it will have repercussions for Hollyhock who will not be able to prove what she is trying to say about Mrs Kan.

7. The phrase that tells us that the boys might resort to physical violence is: 'cracked his knuckles meaningfully'.

The School Outing (page 107)
Questions
1. The class outing has been delayed because the coach has not turned up.
2. The children are supposed to be going to the Stone Age Village at Wendlebury.
3. Ella Jenkins goes to the school office to check that she has booked the coach and to check that the booking fee was paid.
4. Ella thinks that Maisie Gordon is a dear but she has terrible memory lapses and can be a bit slow.
5. Thirty eight children are going on the trip.
6. The coach driver explains that he was delayed due to a flat tyre outside the depot.
7. The further problems Ella experiences are that they are going the wrong way for Wendlebury and she finds out that they are going to Manchester.
8. A requisition form is a form that is used in order to book something like a trip or piece of equipment.
9. To be in a fever of impatience means that you are really desperate for what you want to do to happen and that you can barely contain yourself.

Word work
Rigid – when something is stiff or inflexible
Memory lapses – when someone keeps forgetting things
Risk assessment – before going on an outing, a school will look at the place they are going to visit and see how dangerous or risky it is to go there and minimise any risks by taking action to reduce the possible dangers.
Triumphantly – to be filled with great success

Extension work
1. Mrs Minenski – firm and very on the ball when it comes to understanding what the children might be up to, takes control of situations quickly and deals with them firmly. Maisie Gordon – nice person but forgetful, perhaps a little slow on the uptake. If she has to hoist herself from a chair it means that she might be quite a large individual. She works very slowly and does not look properly through things which means that mistakes are probably made often. We are told she is a cheery woman.
2. We know that Polly is up to mischief because Mrs Minenski is eyeing her beadily which means that she has been alerted to some problem and we are told that Polly is holding a pot of glue.
3. The formal paperwork that Ella has completed is a form for the sandwiches, a risk assessment form, a list of the children going on the trip, a form saying where they are going, a medical details form and the coach requisition form.
4. I think that Ella forces a smile on her face to try and show that she is not worried or flustered by the situation and that she has all the details under control.
5. We know that the trip is not taking place in winter because we are told that it is a bright sunny spring day, perfect for a visit to the Stone Age Village.
6. The phrase that tells us that the school is not a rural one is 'rumbling out of the school gates and through the main town.' OR 'As they made their way through the town …' AND 'It would be nice to get into the countryside.'
7. If the coach had failed to turn up completely I think Ella would have faced 38 disappointed children, the parent helpers would have been very unhappy as their time would have been wasted and it would make the school look inefficient, it would have made Ella look incompetent, she would have had to ring the Stone Age Village and explain what had happened, they would have missed their tour of the village for which they had already paid.

The Viking Raid (page 111)
Questions
1. Knor hates the Vikings because they attack his land and his people, they have burnt his home split his family apart and taken his five year old sister to be a slave.
2. The Saxons have taken Ragsson prisoner. He is the son of Raghelm and he has been able to give them information about the Vikings.
3. Knor's plan is to wreck Raghelm's boat so that he cannot give chase or leave the land, then use one of the other boats to sail and rescue Thyle his sister.
4. Filgar is the chief of the Saxon village.
5. From the passage we learn that Ragsson is a coward and a vile, skulking creature. He is clearly unpleasant and vengeful because he promises them that his father will slaughter them all.
6. Raghelm has become complacent because he thinks that there will not be much resistance to his warriors and that he will be able to attack and plunder the village easily. Due to this, he has only brought a handful of men with

him rather than a larger army to attack.

7. Knor calls Raggin a true friend because he is prepared to leave his home and risk his life in order to help Knor to rescue his sister even though they might both fail.

Word work
Predicted – to foretell what might happen
Slavery – to take someone and use them as unpaid labour without any freedom
Foolhardy – foolish
Rudder – flat piece of wood hinged to the boat's stern in order to steer
Nimbly – to move with agility

Extension work
1. The wise woman makes the sign of protection over Knor because she realises what his intentions are and it is her way of giving her blessing and protection.
2. It is important to Knor to damage Raghelm's boat so that he is unable to follow them and give chase and it will give the Saxons a chance to capture or kill him.
3. A sense of urgency is conveyed in the passage through sentences which convey how the characters are feeling and through descriptive words that describe the Vikings brutality and their impact on the Saxons. This gives us a sense of urgency because we know that everything they do has to be quick and secretive if they are to live. The sentences are also short and punchy.
4. The major themes are that of revenge by the Vikings because we are told Raghelm will return to rescue his son, there is also the revenge that Knor plans in order to rescue his sister because he damages the Vikings' boat. Another major theme is that of loyalty to one's family as

Knor prepares to risk his life in order to rescue his sister. Another theme is that of teamwork for the Saxons all work together in order to ready themselves against the Vikings. We are told that the Saxons have all gathered in their meeting hut to discuss what to do.

5. (Sentences will vary according to what each child chooses.)
6. I think that Knor's fear gives way to rage because he remembers all the terrible things that the Vikings have done to his family and his people and therefore he is no longer afraid but angry at their destruction.
7. The women and children have already left the village in order to hide and keep away from the Vikings so that they cannot be killed or captured as slaves.
8. We know that Raghelm will not be lenient because we are told that he will slaughter them all and that no one will live to tell of their vengeance.

The Snagrond *(page 115)*
Questions
1. Flint and his men are waiting on Skullbone Island.
2. They are waiting for the arrival of Scrawkins.
3. Scrawkins is a pirate.
4. Scrawkins has no fear of storms, he thrives in storms and uses the elements to his advantage.
5. Flint does not allow Whelkin to go with him because he wants him to stay behind and see that the men carry out his orders.
6. The Snagrond is a huge bird-like creature with wings and a beak.
7. The plans are to release some fireballs which will set Scrawkins' ship alight, they will also release some logs which will tumble down the hillside crushing any enemy people coming up the hill.

These tactics are being used to keep the enemy pinned down on the lower part of the hill which gives Flint a chance to invoke the Snagrond.

Word work
Invoked – summoned by special powers
Countless – many
Musket – old-fashioned form of gun
Enterprise – a bold or difficult undertaking
Scourge – a terror

Extension work
1. We learn that Flint is a good Captain because he has planned his tactics carefully and has the respect of Whelkin. We know that he is a stern Captain who expects his orders to be followed implicitly and not disobeyed. He is also prepared to take huge risks if the occasion warrants it, in this case, the invocation of the Snagrond. He also comes across as an inventive individual who uses his environment to help him with his endeavours, namely the logs and the cave and the fireballs. We know that he must be fairly intelligent and well read because he is able to read the invocation and summon the Snagrond. He is also brave because he fights Scrawkins in hand to hand combat even though Scrawkins is the better swordsman.
2. (A personal response is needed for this question so answers will vary.)
3. The weather plays an important part in the story because it is very much as if it is a reflection of Scrawkins' anger as he comes on the hunt for Flint. The storm is also important because the wind and rain mask the men on the island and the seas will be difficult for Scrawkins to navigate. The storm rages as the two men battle with

Brilliant Activities for Reading Comprehension, Year 6
© Charlotte Makhlouf and Brilliant Publications Limited

each other and it is as if the elements are rumbling in response to the words of the invocation that is summoning the Snagrond. The weather also seems to be a huge supporter of Scrawkins and it could be said that it is supporting and helping him because we have been told that the weather embraces him and makes him its own.

4. The methods of attack Flint uses are the logs being rolled down the hill to maim and crush, the fireballs to set the ship on fire and the invocation of the Snagrond who will probably kill Scrawkins. Flint also uses his sword to fight Scrawkins. His men also have muskets to fire upon the enemy.

5. The reasons given for leaving Turtle Island are that the thatched huts on the island would have given them no protection against Scrawkins or the weather.

6. We know that storms present no difficulty to Scrawkins because we are told that he thrives on them and uses the elements to his advantage. The wind and the rain seem to embrace him and make him their own.

7. The words or phrases that tell us that fate has helped Flint are: 'The cave had been a godsend'. 'Flint felt a surge of power rush through him.' (Other phrases may be chosen but they should be justified as to why they are fateful.)

Virus on Space Station (page 119)
Questions
1. The first people caught the disease at the Sigfelm Delta Colony.
2. The disease is alarming because people die very quickly once they get the disease.
3. The main symptoms of the disease are wheezing and constriction of the lungs, tiny blisters at the ends of the fingers and toes which cause irritation and intense burning all over the body. People then become cold and are shocked into a coma and then death.
4. Hope is being placed on the small boy because he has been in touch with the disease and yet he is not affected by it. If he is immune to the disease he may have something special which the doctors can find out about and use to help other people who have the disease by producing a vaccine.
5. Travel has been suspended so that the disease does not spread and it can be contained.
6. Doctor Jasmine Wetherby believes in a conspiracy theory in which she thinks that the disease has been deliberately introduced to the holiday centre with the aim of killing people and producing a serious epidemic.
7. Two sentences which I feel convey the seriousness of the situation are: 'At present there is no vaccine, and no guaranteed cure and the disease is spreading'. And, 'The government has instituted emergency procedures in order to halt the spread of this unseen killer.' OR 'Meanwhile our hope is placed on one small boy and his doctors'.

Word work
Guaranteed – answer for fulfilment, a giver of security or guarantee
Vaccine – a substance that is used for inoculation against a disease
Immunity – to have something within your body that prevents you from getting a disease
Evidence – information to prove that something has or has not been done or something like a vaccine actually works
Critical – very serious situation
Mutating – to change
Postpone – to put something on hold or to stop something from happening until a different date

Extension work
1. Answers will vary about what emergency procedures should be followed, some guidelines are: breathing masks should be worn at all times when outside, all public buildings should have special antibacterial hand washes to help stop the spread of the disease, the army or police might be used to ensure that people do not leave cities and therefore spread the disease, emergency tented hospitals and walk in centres might be erected to give quick assistance to people who are unwell on the streets, pharmaceutical companies could be given specific instructions to use all their resources to find a vaccine as fast as possible, clever scientists could find a way of giving false information to the bad bacteria in the disease to stop it from mutating effectively.
2–5. (Require a personal and imaginative response to the questions therefore answers will vary.)
6 This tells you that their initial ideas were very confident in so far as they anticipated being able to bring the virus under control and thereby find a vaccine to halt it. They might have also thought that the virus was not as deadly as people said, however, they have been proved wrong.

Lightning Source UK Ltd.
Milton Keynes UK
UKHW050625210322
400374UK00001B/1

9 781783 170753